Can Do

Problem-solving

Year 5 / P6

Teacher's Book

Sarah Foster

Lynsey Ankers

Published in 2004 by:
Nelson Thornes Ltd
Delta Place
27 Bath Road
CHELTENHAM
GL53 7TH
United Kingdom

04 05 06 07 08 / 10 9 8 7 6 5 4 3 2 1

A catalogue record for this book is available from the British Library

ISBN 0-7487-7741-5

Illustrations by Jo Taylor and Aetos Ltd
Page make-up by Aetos Ltd

Printed in Great Britain by Antony Rowe

Acknowledgements
Bob Owen for preparation of the Problems Bank questions
Rae Cook and Margaret McDougall for original ideas

Contents

Can Do Problem-solving provides a structured whole-school approach to developing the teaching of problem-solving in mathematics. With materials written for Years 1 to 6, it addresses problem-solving in line with current developments from the Primary National Strategy. The resource introduces and develops a systematic approach to problem-solving embodied in a 'Five Steps' process and introduces and develops a range of strategies for children to use when solving problems. Both the Five Steps process and the range of strategies are described fully in the section on 'An approach to problem-solving'. The problems have been carefully selected to ensure that children have experience of a wide variety of types of problems and that they are given the opportunity to consolidate skills regularly when they meet similar problems as they progress through the school.

An approach to problem-solving

Problem-solving is a key skill, not only in mathematics, but right across the curriculum. In order to develop skills and become successful problem-solvers children need to be provided with strategies to do this. One of the skills that they will need in any problem-solving activity is the ability to work systematically and this is embodied in the 'Five Steps' process described below. Through the materials, this process is first introduced and then developed. As children become familiar with the procedure, it may not be necessary to refer to it in every lesson.

The Five Steps process

The Five Step process is a systematic approach to problem-solving and can be used for solving any problem.

Five Steps to Problem-solving

report and record

consider

experiment

choose a strategy

read and think

5

4

3

2

1

1 Read and think

The first step involves the reading of the problem and identifying the question. Essential information should be identified and extracted. Children should also consider whether there is sufficient information to solve the problem. Misleading or unnecessary information should also be discarded at this point. A starting point may also be identified.

2 Choose a strategy

The second step involves choosing appropriate strategies, which will help solve the problem. Children are introduced to these gradually in Years 1 to 3 and after that they will be practised in selecting appropriate strategies. They will also come to understand that a combination of strategies will be used for many problems and that different strategies might be used at different stages of the problem. It is also important that children recognise that different starting points and therefore different strategies will be utilised by some children when tackling the same problem. The nine strategies are explained in full in the section on problem-solving strategies.

3 Experiment

The third step involves children using their chosen strategies to solve the problem. They should be encouraged to work systematically as they approach the problem. Several different strategies could be used at this stage; moving from one to another is acceptable and part of the process.

4 Consider

During the problem-solving process children should review their progress and consider how to continue. A change of direction and strategies may be necessary if their chosen strategy does not help. At this point it is likely that their thinking would turn to methods of recording their initial findings.

5 Report and record

Children are encouraged to record as they work through the problem. The reporting stage will involve identifying the solution and explaining their reasoning. They should also check that the answer is reasonable and answers the question. Reflecting on the strategies used is also important.

The problem-solving strategies

The nine problem-solving strategies are introduced over the first three years of the programme, building into a repertoire of strategies that the child can draw on. In many problems there will be more than one strategy that can be used to help solve the problem and the strategies should not be seen in isolation. Children should be encouraged to see the links between the strategies and that by implementing one strategy another could also be used. The strategies as described here are in no particular order.

Problem-solving Strategies

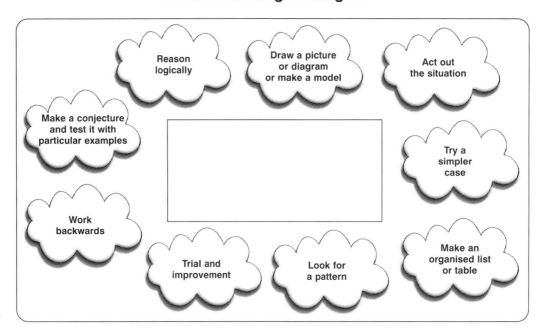

Try a simpler case

Children may sometimes find it useful to make problems simpler. This strategy is particularly helpful where the numbers used or the number of combinations are large. They could reduce the range of numbers involved or decrease the numbers of items involved. Working with the simpler representation of a problem may help them identify what operation to use or how a pattern develops.

Act out the situation

This strategy will help with the visualisation of the problem and the exploration of a number of possibilities leading to the solution. Mathematical apparatus, other objects, scraps of paper and even the children themselves can be used in the modelling of the problem. Many children will use this as an initial strategy.

Draw a picture or a diagram or make a model

This strategy will help with the visualisation of the problem and allow different possibilities to be explored. They will help the child understand and manipulate the data. Using diagrams is almost a necessity for some problems, particularly those that involve mapping. Diagrams are extensively used in problems where 'reason logically' is the main strategy used.

Make an organised list or table

Using a table or organised list is an effective way to put data into an orderly arrangement. It will help children keep a track of data more easily, spot missing data and identify duplicated data. It is essential when children are asked to find all the possibilities in a problem. When data is organised into a list or table, patterns are easily identified. An organised list can provide a systematic way of recording calculations made with given data or recording combinations of given items. This strategy is often used in conjunction with and as a development of other strategies.

Look for a pattern

A pattern is a regular systematic repetition in data. By identifying a pattern the child can predict what will happen the 'next time' and subsequently. Looking for a pattern is a very important strategy and often linked to the 'make an organised list or table' strategy. Often the child can solve the problem just by identifying the pattern. In other problems the pattern has to be extended and generalisations made before the solution can be reached. For older children the 'look for a pattern' strategy is developed into a written generalisation, applying and extending it to predict the next few terms in the sequence.

Trial and improvement

When children use this strategy they initially make an estimate at the answer, based on the data given in the problem. They then test to see whether it is correct and adjust the estimate according to the result and then repeat the procedure. In this way they gradually come closer and closer to a solution. On occasion this is the sole strategy for solving the problem. This strategy can be used to get started and before identifying another strategy. It is also used where the child is asked to find one solution but not all the possible solutions. It is particularly helpful when the problem presents so many pieces of data that making an organised list becomes a major task.

Make a conjecture and test it with particular examples

This strategy is used to prove statements. It can be used to identify that something happens in every case. It is also used to test two or more situations where a choice needs to be made. It is often used as a check when a generalisation has been made in the problem-solving process.

Work backwards

To solve certain types of problem children will need to make a series of calculations based on data presented in the problem. These types of problems necessitate children starting with the data presented at the end of the series of computations and then working backwards to data presented at the beginning in order to solve the problem. This strategy often requires inverse operations to be used in the calculations.

Reason logically

Logical reasoning is used in every problem as the child goes through the problem-solving process. It is also used specifically in the types of problem where the solution can be worked out by examining a set of conditional statements, e.g.: If … then. The child can work his or her way through the statements in a systematic way, looking for relationships or patterns in the information or conditions. The data given in these problems can often be displayed in a chart or matrix or other diagram.

The materials

There are three elements for each year of *Can Do Problem-solving:*
- the *Whiteboard CD-ROM*
- the *Teacher's Book*
- the *Resources CD-ROM*.

These have been designed to be as flexible as possible and offer individual schools different models of use: the three components fit together to offer a comprehensive programme which will provide continuity and progression in problem-solving.

The Whiteboard CD-ROM

This contains nine main lessons for the teacher to use with the whole class to model the problem-solving process. Full lesson plans are included on the CD-ROM to make it a self-contained resource as well being integrated with the rest of the materials. The lessons that are contained on it are searchable by NNS link or by problem-solving strategy. If the *Resources CD-ROM* is installed there is a direct link into the follow-up problems related to that unit.

The Teacher's Book

The book is divided into two sections.

Section 1 – Problem-solving Units

This is divided into nine units. Each unit provides one main problem and two follow-up problems. Each unit focuses on a specific type of problem and has a variety of problem-solving strategies related to it. Each main problem is accompanied by two lesson plans, one for use with an interactive whiteboard (Lesson A) and one for use when an interactive whiteboard is not available (Lesson B). The two follow-up main problems in each unit are designed to provide further opportunities for children to apply similar approaches.

- Each unit begins with a Unit Overview page that provides the NNS links, the problem-solving strategies used in the problem, an overview of resources and the follow-up problems.

- A full lesson plan is provided for the main lesson. These lessons are designed to be used during a whole class session and the lesson plans provide suggestions for using an interactive approach to problem-solving. The structure of the lessons follows the 'Five Steps' process to demonstrate a systematic approach. There are ideas to support less able children and there is an extension to most problems that can be used if required. The solutions are fully explained with notes for the teacher in many cases. Resource Sheets for use in the main lessons are also provided in the *Teacher's Book* and are designed to help children implement the problem-solving strategies.

- Follow-up problems. There are two of these in a unit, and each is accompanied by lesson notes. These follow-up problems can be used immediately after a main problem to reinforce the approaches and strategies used. Each follow-up problem is differentiated at three levels. The core activity presents the main problem. The support level of the activity either simplifies the problem, or offers support in solving the main problem. The extension activity either provides a harder version of the core problem or offers a 'what if …' scenario for children who complete the main problem. The Scope and Sequence chart on page xi indicates how the problems relate to the *National Numeracy Strategy Framework for Teaching Mathematics*. It also indicates which problem-solving strategies are addressed in each problem.

Section 2 – Problems Bank

The Problems Bank provides a bank of problems for the teacher to select from. These problems include a wide variety of types of problem including 'word problems', and many will provide opportunities to apply specific mathematical knowledge and skills in new contexts. The problems can be matched to the National Numeracy Strategy's Framework Objectives using the grid at the beginning of the section or alternatively by accessing the easy-to-use search facility on the *Resources CD-ROM*. Each problem is listed using the title, NNS link and the solution.

The Resources CD-ROM

The *Resources CD-ROM* contains three differentiated resource sheets for each of the follow-up problems as well as pupil cards for each of the problems in the Problems Bank of the *Teacher's Book*. The full contents are listed and matched to the order in the *Teacher's Book*. Problems can also be searched by selecting a particular NNS link. To print any of the pupil cards simply select the title and click on the Print button. Similarly, to print the resource sheets select the follow-up problem required. This will give a choice of the core (Resource Sheet **a**), support (Resource Sheet **b**) or extension (Resource Sheet **c**) – simply select the one that is required and click on the Print button.

Using the materials in the classroom

The materials have been designed to be as flexible as possible to fit into existing planning, and can be used to plan problem-solving activities in different ways.

The problem-solving units

The problem-solving units could be used in two main ways in the classroom and the lesson plans in the *Teacher's Book* can be adapted for both approaches.

Approach A

Introduce one of the main problems in an initial whole class session, using the 'Read and think' screen from the whiteboard or by writing the problem on the board. Work through the whole of a problem as a teacher-led activity, using the ideas in the lesson plans to demonstrate the problem-solving process and the implementation and development of strategies. Allow children time to work in pairs or small groups, particularly in the 'Experiment' phase of the process. This time can be used to support individuals who experience difficulties. Draw the class together to share the 'Report and record' findings. Discuss the solution and the strategies used. Move to the extension if required.

One of the follow-up problems can then be used to allow children to work independently. The differentiated resource sheets can be used to provide an appropriate level of the problem.

Approach B

Introduce one of the main problems in an initial whole class session, using the 'Read and think' screen from the whiteboard or by writing the problem on the board. Discuss the 'Five Steps' process and the strategies that could be used for the problem. Allow children to continue work in pairs or small groups, and provide support if required. Draw children together to discuss solutions in a plenary session. Return to the whiteboard activity or board to model the different aspects of the problem-solving process and the strategies used. Stress the stages and steps within the process that the children have used and how these could be refined when attempting similar problems in the future. Use the extension activity to extend children's thinking.

A follow-up problem can be used to provide another opportunity to apply and refine the strategies used.

The lesson plans stress the importance of interaction through questioning and discussion; suggestions for interaction that involves both teacher/child and between children are included. Children are also encouraged to explain their reasoning as they work through the problems.

The Problems Bank

The Problems Bank provides a wide range of types of problem including 'word problems'. Some of these in the Year 5 materials can be used with a calculator and this is shown by the use of a calculator icon beside the problem. The problems can be dipped into whenever problem-solving activities are required. The problems are referenced both by problem-solving objective and by mathematical content so they are ideal for integrating into coverage of a particular objective. They can be used to provide additional contexts for making use of and applying skills learnt. Many of the problems included ask children to explain their reasoning.

Many of the problems are structured so that they become more challenging as the parts of the problem are worked through. It may be appropriate to use only the first or first and second parts of the problem with some children. The structure provides extension work via the same problem for more able children. Children should be encouraged to show their working and reasoning whether this be in figures, words, diagrams, lists or tables.

Additional Resources

Think Maths CD-ROM

Think Maths CD-ROM offers a useful accompaniment to *Can Do Problem-solving*, providing the opportunity for continuing professional development in the key problem-solving skills and strategies.

The CD-ROM has been published by Nelson Thornes in conjunction with BEAM (ISBN 0-7487-8609-0). For further information about this product, contact Nelson Thornes on 01242-267280 or visit the web site at www.nelsonthornes.com/primary

Scope and Sequence Chart

Column key (problems listed left → right as printed; **bold** = Unit title):

#	Unit / Problem
1	The Rides
2	Tower Heights Prices
3	**9 Tower Heights**
4	Big Burgers
5	Rabbit Hutch
6	**8 The Party**
7	The Bus Station
8	Old Macdonald
9	**7 The Airport**
10	The Long Jump
11	The Computer Game
12	**6 The Rucksack**
13	Number Puzzles
14	PIN Number
15	**5 Craig's Telephone Number**
16	Chime Bars
17	Ice Creams
18	**4 Aliens**
19	The Big Top
20	Netball Practice
21	**3 The Football League**
22	Ages
23	Christmas Cards
24	**2 The Treasure Game**
25	Neighbours
26	The Wedding Plan
27	**1 The Table Plan**

NNS links

Criterion	Problems marked (●)
Choose and use appropriate number operations and appropriate ways of calculating to solve problems	1, 2, 3, 4, 5, 6, 13, 22, 23
Explain methods and reasoning about numbers, orally and in writing	1, 2, 3, 4, 5, 6, 13, 14, 15, 16, 19, 22, 23, 26
Make and investigate a general statement about familiar numbers or shapes by finding examples that satisfy it	—
Express a relationship in words, orally and in writing	19, 20, 21
Solve mathematical problems or puzzles, recognise and explain patterns and relationships, generalise and predict. Suggest extensions by asking 'What if …?'	4, 5, 6, 7, 8, 9, 10, 13, 14, 15, 16, 17, 18, 19, 20, 21, 22, 23, 24, 25, 26
Use all four operations to solve word problems involving numbers in 'real life'	12, 14, 15, 22, 23
Use all four operations to solve word problems involving money	2
Use all four operations to solve word problems involving length, mass or capacity	3, 10
Use all four operations to solve word problems involving time	1, 7, 8, 11
Reason about shape	—

Problem-solving strategy

Strategy	Problems marked (●)
Act out the situation	6, 19, 20, 21, 22
Look for a pattern	18, 19, 20
Try a simpler case	18, 19, 20
Draw a picture or diagram or make a model	3, 11, 18, 19, 23
Make an organised list or table	7, 8, 9, 16, 17, 18, 19, 20
Trial and improvement	4, 5, 6, 10, 11, 12, 13, 14, 15
Make a conjecture and test it with particular examples	1, 2, 3
Work backwards	22, 23, 24
Reason logically	3, 7, 8, 9, 10, 11, 12, 13, 15, 16, 22, 23, 25, 26

Can Do

Problem-solving

SECTION 1

Problem-solving Units

Unit **1** *THE TABLE PLAN*

▶ *Problem*

The seating plan at the table in the classroom is to be changed.
The teacher's instructions are:
- Sean is to keep the same seat.
- Martin and Harry are not to sit together.
- Shannon is to sit nearest to the teacher.
- Aasia and Max must sit together, with Aasia next to Shannon.
- Lloyd is to sit next to Harry.
- Erin is to sit next to Shannon.

NNS links	Solve mathematical problems or puzzles, recognise and explain patterns and relationships, generalise and predict. Suggest extensions by asking 'What if …?' Explain methods and reasoning about numbers, orally and in writing.
Problem-solving strategies	▪ Reason logically ▪ Act out the situation
Overview	This problem encourages the development of logical reasoning to solve problems and the use of 'acting out' scenarios to improve understanding of the problem and work towards a solution. The problem needs to be taken step by step using the various 'clues' and the solution reviewed at regular intervals.
Resources	**Lesson A** Interactive whiteboard *Can Do Problem-solving Year 5/P6 Whiteboard CD-ROM* Individual pupil whiteboards and pens Resource Sheet 2 Table Plan and Names **Lesson B** General Resource Sheet A and General Resource Sheet B – enlarged or copied onto OHT Resource Sheet 1 Table Plan and Clues. Copy on different coloured card and cut out individual labels – one per pair of children Resource Sheet 2 Table Plan and Names. Copy on different coloured card and cut out individual labels – one per pair of children Individual pupil whiteboards and pens
Follow-up problems	The Wedding Plan Neighbours

....

▶ *Introduction*

Begin by revising the problem-solving process. Click on the Five steps button to show this screen on the whiteboard.

Read and think

SCREEN 1
This shows a visual of the table plan.

Show The Table Plan problem on the whiteboard. Ensure that the children understand that the teacher is Mr Jarvis. Prompt for understanding:

What information are you given?

What information do you require to solve the problem?

Allow time for the children to think independently first and then ask them to discuss with a partner how they would go about solving the problem.

Choose a strategy

Revise the nine problem-solving strategies by clicking on the Strategies button on the screen.

Which strategies would be appropriate for this problem and which would not?

Allow a couple of minutes for the children to discuss the range of suitable strategies with their partners. Appropriate strategies should include 'reason logically' and 'act out the situation'.

How would you organise the information you are given? (Perhaps decide on the 'priority order.')

How might you act out the problem? (Could act out physically or using name cards around a table.)

Experiment

SCREEN 2
Drag and drop the clues to rearrange them in priority order. This information is carried forward to Screen 3.

Allow the children time to discuss each piece of information with their partners.

Ask the children whether any of the clues could be used straight away. Take examples, e.g.

'Shannon sits nearest the teacher.'

'Erin sits next to Shannon.'

Identify these as offering exact information and reorder the clues on the whiteboard.

Take feedback on the clues, sorting the information that is useful from that which would be useful later.

Allow children time to experiment using name cards made from Resource Sheet 2.

Consider

SCREEN 3
Drag and drop the pupils to new positions. Click on Done to activate the Solution screen.

Draw the children together to discuss progress. Allow the children to show partial solutions on the whiteboard. Invite individuals to show their progress on the whiteboard, verbalising their reasoning as they do so. Offer hints if there is a common problem. Allow further time to complete the problem or continue the process on the whiteboard.

Report and record

Look back to the problem. Ask for a solution to the original problem. Ask individual children to explain their answers in words and using Screens 2 and 3.

Does this solution answer the question?

How can we check that we have solved the problem?

What information was essential for you to solve the problem?

Give the children the opportunity to evaluate the strategies they have used to solve the problem.

Would you use the same strategies if you had to solve similar problems in the future?

Is there more than one solution to the problem? Encourage children to look for more than one solution to the problem.

▶▶ Extension

EXTENSION SCREEN
This has the same functionality as Screen 2.

On the Extension screen the children are challenged to write another set of clues for the problem. Some sets of clues could be tried out on screen.

▶▶ Support

● Provide name cards (Resource Sheet 2) so that the children can act out the problem around a table.

● Support the children in establishing which order to use each piece of information.

Solution

Main   There are four solutions.

Extension   Open-ended.

	Lloyd	Max	Aasia	
Harry				Shannon Mr Jarvis
	Sean	Martin	Erin	

	Harry	Max	Aasia	
Lloyd				Shannon Mr Jarvis
	Sean	Martin	Erin	

	Lloyd	Harry	Erin	
Martin				Shannon Mr Jarvis
	Sean	Max	Aasia	

	Lloyd	Martin	Erin	
Harry				Shannon Mr Jarvis
	Sean	Max	Aasia	

. . . .

▶ *Introduction*

Begin by revising the problem-solving process. Display this by using an enlarged version of General Resource Sheet A or copying it onto OHT.

Read and think

Write The Table Plan problem on the flip chart. If desired, Resource Sheet 1 can be enlarged to show the seating plan and the clues. Give the children time to read the problem line by line. Prompt for understanding:

What information are you given?

What information do you need in order to solve the problem?

Allow time for the children to think independently first and then ask them to discuss with a partner how they would go about solving the problem.

Choose a strategy

Display the nine problem-solving strategies by enlarging General Resource Sheet B or copying it onto OHT.

Which strategies would be appropriate for this problem and which would not?

Allow a couple of minutes for children to discuss the range of suitable strategies with their partners. Appropriate strategies should include 'reason logically' and 'act out the situation'.

How would you organise the information you are given? (Perhaps decide on the 'priority order.')

How might you act out the problem? (Could act out physically or use the name cards made from Resource Sheet 2.)

Experiment

Allow children time to discuss each piece of information with their partners. Give the children time to put the clues into order.

Supply each pair with name labels and a blank table plan (copied from Resource Sheet 2). Encourage the children to act out the situation by positioning (and repositioning) the name labels around the table, working through the clues systematically.

continued

Consider

Draw the children together to review progress. Ask the children which clues could be used straight away. Take examples, e.g.

'Shannon sits nearest the teacher.'

'Erin sits next to Shannon.'

Identify these as offering exact information and highlight these clues on the flip chart or Resource Sheet.

Allow time for further explanation if necessary or move on to Report and record.

Report and record

Look back to the problem. There are four possible solutions to this problem (see Solution on page 8). Ask individual children to explain their solution in words and using the flip chart if necessary.

Does this solution answer the question?

How can we check that we have solved the problem?

Give the children the opportunity to evaluate the strategies they have used to solve the problem.

Would you use the same strategies if you had to solve similar problems in the future?

▶▶ Extension

Amend the instructions so that the problem has more than one possible solution.

What information could be missed out and the problem still solved?

Children could be challenged to write a set of clues to place the children around the table. Some of their clues could be tried out in a plenary session.

▶▶ Support

● Support the children in acting out the problem. Ask the children to explain their reasons for positioning each pupil.

● Support the children in establishing which order to use each piece of information.

Solution

Main   There are four solutions.

| Lloyd | Max | Aasia |

| Harry | | Shannon | Mr Jarvis |

| Sean | Martin | Erin |

| Harry | Max | Aasia |

| Lloyd | | Shannon | Mr Jarvis |

| Sean | Martin | Erin |

| Lloyd | Harry | Erin |

| Martin | | Shannon | Mr Jarvis |

| Sean | Max | Aasia |

| Lloyd | Martin | Erin |

| Harry | | Shannon | Mr Jarvis |

| Sean | Max | Aasia |

Extension   Open-ended

▶ Problem

Michelle and Wan are getting married.
They have to arrange where everyone is going to sit for the celebration meal.
Nicky has chosen her own seat.
John and George are not sitting together.
Evie is to sit nearest to the bride and groom.
Kim and Miles are to sit together, with Miles next to Evie.
Ian is to sit next to George who is to sit next to Kim.
Darcey is to sit next to Evie.

NNS links	Solve mathematical problems or puzzles, recognise and explain patterns and relationships, generalise and predict. Suggest extensions by asking 'What if …?'

Problem-solving strategies	▧ Reason logically ▧ Act out the situation ▧ Draw a picture or diagram or make a model

Overview	This problem will provide an opportunity for children to reason logically and is an ideal follow-up to The Table Plan. Resource Sheet **a** could be used to provide the children with visual support. Encourage the children to make name cards for the guests. Draw the children together to establish progress being made as the problem is being solved. This will give the children the opportunity to share strategies and evaluate the strategies they are using. Three differentiated resource sheets are provided on the *Resources CD-ROM*. These can be used to support this activity.

▶▶ Core

Children use Resource Sheet **a** to solve the problem.

Solution:

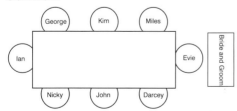

▶▶ Support

The problem on Resource Sheet **b** offers a simplified version of the problem. Some of the guests have already been placed and the clues are presented in the order they should be considered.

Solution: The solution is the same as for the main problem.

▶▶ Extension

Resource Sheet **c** asks the children to solve the main problem. It then asks them to write a different set of clues, which will give the same solution.

Solution: The solution is the same as for the main problem. For the extension activity children's work will vary.

▶ **Problem**

The building plan for a new street shows where each family will live.
None of the houses have numbers.
Using the clues, can you place the correct families in their new homes?

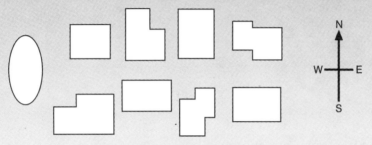

The Robson family and the Smith family live next door to each other.
The Green family lives next to Mr and Mrs Jones and Miss Brown.
Mr and Mrs Jones live next to the pond.
Miss Hughes lives next to Miss Brown and opposite the Shah family who live on the south side of the street.
Mr Wilson lives opposite the house next to the pond.
The Robson family lives next to Mr Wilson.

NNS links	Solve mathematical problems or puzzles, recognise and explain patterns and relationships, generalise and predict. Suggest extensions by asking 'What if …?'

Problem-solving strategies	■ Reason logically ■ Act out the situation

Overview	This problem gives children the opportunity to use the strategy to reason logically.

Use Resource Sheet **a** to show the children the problem and ask them what information they are given and what they need to find out in order to solve the problem. Encourage the children to consider the strategies they have used in similar problems. Stress that each clue needs to be looked at carefully and that they should consider at regular intervals where they have placed the families to check that these match the clues they are given.

Three differentiated resource sheets are provided on the *Resources CD-ROM*. These can be used to support this activity.

▶▶ Core

The children use Resource Sheet **a** to solve the problem.

Solution:

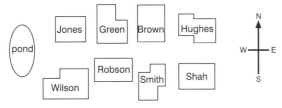

▶▶ Support

Resource Sheet **b** offers a simplified version of the problem with only four houses on the plan. The clues can also be looked at in the order they are given.

Solution:

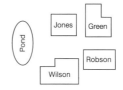

▶▶ Extension

Resource Sheet **c** presents the children with the main problem and then asks them to add two more houses and instructions for someone else to complete the plan.

Solution:
As Resource Sheet **a** with two more houses.

Unit **2** THE TREASURE GAME

▶ *Problem*

Kieran is playing the Treasure Game on his computer.
He collects some gold coins from the mine.
He carries the coins up a ladder to the surface.
On the way up bandits force him to give them half of the gold coins he is carrying.
He is then chased by a monster and drops 15 coins.
When he reaches the top he has 30 gold coins.
How many gold coins did he collect at the start?

NNS links

Solve mathematical problems or puzzles, recognise and explain patterns and relationships, generalise and predict. Suggest extensions by asking 'What if …?'

Explain methods and reasoning about numbers, orally and in writing.

Problem-solving strategies

- Work backwards
- Act out the situation
- Draw a picture or diagram or make a model

Overview

This problem is designed to reinforce the strategy 'work backwards' or using inverse operations to solve a problem. The problem also encourages the children to adopt a systematic approach to identifying the correct starting point for the problem. The children should be encouraged to use a diagram or flow chart to help them to develop this systematic approach.

Resources

Lesson A
Interactive whiteboard
Can Do Problem-solving Year 5/P6 Whiteboard CD-ROM
Individual pupil whiteboards (or paper) and pens

Lesson B
General Resource Sheet A and General Resource Sheet B – enlarge or copy onto OHT
Counters

Follow-up problems

Christmas Cards
Ages

▶ *Introduction*

Begin by revising the problem-solving process. Click on the Five steps button to show this on the whiteboard screen.

Read and think

Show The Treasure Game problem on the whiteboard. Give the children time to read the problem line by line. Ask the children to explain the problem to their partners in their own words. Prompt for understanding:

What information are you given?

What information do you need in order solve the problem?

Ensure that the children are able to identify the key items of information in the problem.

SCREEN 1
Show the problem on the whiteboard. The problem text appears after a short animation, which can be used to set the context for the problem.

Choose a strategy

Review the nine problem-solving strategies by clicking on the Strategies button on the screen. Establish the fact that the children know that Kieran ended up with 30 gold coins and that they need to work backwards to find out how many coins he started with.

Ask the children:

If we want to know how many gold coins Kieran collected at the start, how could we find this out?

Allow time for the children to think independently first and then ask them to discuss with a partner how they would go about solving the problem.

Discuss all the possible options, but try to establish 'work backwards' as the most appropriate strategy to solve this problem.

Experiment

Introduce Screen 2 and set the children a challenge:

You know what happened at the end, but how are you going to find out what happened at the beginning of the game?

Click back onto the initial problem and read through step by step.

Ask children to identify the operations they would use, starting at the bottom:

SCREEN 2
Use the keypad to enter operations and totals in the boxes.

> *collects gold*
>
> *loses half (or ÷ 2)*
>
> *drops 15 (or − 15)*
>
> *arrives with 30.*

Ask children to enter these in the operations boxes. Why can't they solve the problem? Encourage them to think about working backwards and using inverse operations.

continued

Consider

If necessary, prompt the children to draw a diagram or flow chart to help them develop a systematic approach.

Draw children together to discuss how they have solved the problem. Ask individuals to show their working on Screen 2, entering the totals and operation for each stage.

Make sure all the children have at least some form of written explanation and give the children opportunities to modify or redraft their explanations with a partner before taking feedback about the solution. Activate the Solution screen by pressing Done.

Report and record

Look back at the problem.

Has the problem been solved? Does the solution answer the question?

Record the solution on the whiteboard with an explanation of how the solution was achieved – by working backwards and the use of inverse calculations. The Solution screen can be gone through step by step at this stage. Discuss the 'work backwards' strategy. Use the Solution screen to show how the inverse operation is used at each stage. Finally, press Play a second time to show the reverse of the process. Identify any alternative methods of arriving at the solution. Ask the children to explain these methods.

SOLUTION SCREEN
Press Play to show the solution for using the 'work backwards' strategy. Click on Play again to show how this is arrived at.

▶▶ Extension

EXTENSION SCREEN
Draw children together to discuss how they have solved the problem. Ask individuals to show their working on Screen 2, entering the totals and operation for each stage.

The extension provides another problem which will provide further experience of the 'work backwards' strategy.

▶▶ Support
● Help children identify the starting point.
● Discuss the 'work backwards' strategy.

Solution

See also the Solution screen.

Main   90 gold coins.

Extension   140 coins.

Unit 2 LESSON B

▶ **Introduction**

Begin by revising the problem-solving process. Display this by using an enlarged version of General Resource Sheet A or displaying it on OHT.

Read and think

Write The Treasure Game problem on a flip chart. Give the children time to read the problem line by line. Ask each child to explain the problem to a partner in her/his own words. Prompt for understanding:

What information are you given?

What information do you need in order solve the problem?

Ensure that the children are able to identify the key items of information in the problem.

Choose a strategy

Display the nine problem-solving strategies by enlarging General Resource Sheet B. Discuss the strategies that children could use. Suggestions should include 'work backwards' and 'act out the situation'. Establish the fact that the children know that Kieran ended up with 30 gold coins and that they need to work backwards to find out how many coins he started with.

Ask the children:

If we want to know how many gold coins Kieran collected at the start, how could we find this out?

Allow time for the children to think independently first and then ask them to discuss with a partner how they would go about solving the problem.

Discuss all the possible options, but try to establish 'work backwards' as the most appropriate strategy to solve this problem.

Experiment

Set the children a challenge:

You know what happened at the end, but how are you going to find out what happened at the beginning of the game?

Encourage the children to think about inverse operations to solve the problem and about a method of recording the problem. You might also encourage them to make an approximation of the starting number of coins and then to act out the situation using counters.

continued

Consider

If necessary, prompt the children to draw a diagram or flow chart to help them develop a systematic approach. Prompt for the different stages of the problem, i.e.

collects gold

loses half (or ÷2)

drops 15 (or –15)

arrives with 30.

So to find the solution children can use the inverse operation.

The Solution below suggests one possible format for recording the work. This might be used after the children have discussed their possible solutions with their partners. Make sure all the children have at least some form of written explanation and give the children opportunities to modify or redraft their explanations with a partner before revealing the prepared diagram.

Report and record

Look back at the problem.

Has the problem been solved? Does the solution answer the question?

Record the solution on the flip chart with an explanation of how the solution was achieved – by working backwards and the use of inverse calculations. Identify any alternative methods of arriving at the solution. Ask the children to explain these methods. For example:

How did you act out the situation?

How close was your approximation? How did you test it?

▶▶ Extension

Another similar problem could be posed. 'Kieran plays again and finishes with 30 coins. This time bandits take 20 of the coins. He is then chased by a dragon and drops $\frac{3}{4}$ of the coins. How many did he have to start with?'

▶▶ Support

- Help children identify the starting point.
- Discuss the 'work backwards' strategy.

Solution

Main 90 gold coins.

$$\boxed{90} \xrightarrow{\boxed{\div 2}} \boxed{45} \xrightarrow{\boxed{-15}} \boxed{30}$$

Extension 140 coins.

▶ *Problem*

Bethany has bought a packet of Christmas cards to send to all of her friends.
She writes half of the packet for her friends at school.
She sends 14 to her friends at dancing class.
She has 6 left in the packet.
How many Christmas cards were there in the packet to start with?

NNS links	Choose and use appropriate number operations and appropriate ways of calculating to solve problems.
	Use all four operations to solve word problems involving numbers in 'real life'.

Problem-solving strategies	▨ Work backwards
	▨ Reason logically
	▨ Draw a picture or diagram or make a model

Overview	In this problem the children will be using different number operations to calculate how many Christmas cards were contained in the packet. Encourage the children to consider how they solved The Treasure Game or similar problems they have worked with and strategies they have used. The most effective strategy for this problem is to work backwards.
	Three differentiated resource sheets are provided on the *Resources CD-ROM*. These can be used to support this activity.

▷▷ *Core*

The main problem is presented to the children on Resource Sheet **a**.

Solution: 40 Christmas cards were in the pack to start with.

▷▷ *Support*

A simpler version of the problem is presented on Resource Sheet **b**.

Solution: 20 cards.

▷▷ *Extension*

A more challenging version of the problem using larger numbers and more stages to the problem is presented on Resource Sheet **c**.

Solution: 112 cards.

▶ Problem

Abigail is younger than Peter, who is 19 years old.
Three years ago her age was one quarter of Peter's age.
How old is she now?

NNS links

Choose and use appropriate number operations and appropriate ways of calculating to solve problems.

Use all four operations to solve word problems involving numbers in 'real life'.

Explain methods and reasoning about numbers, orally and in writing.

Problem-solving strategies

- Work backwards
- Reason logically

Overview

Encourage the children to consider similar problems they have solved and strategies they have used in order to solve them. The main strategy here will be to work backwards from the starting point of Peter's age. Children should be encouraged to record their thinking as they attempt to solve the problem. This problem could be the focus of a plenary session.

Three differentiated resource sheets are provided on the *Resources CD-ROM*. These can be used to support this activity.

▶▶ Core

The main problem is presented to the children on Resource Sheet **a**.

Solution: 7 years.

▶▶ Support

A simpler version of the problem is provided on Resource Sheet **b**. For children who are struggling, establish the starting point as Peter's age now.

Solution: 7 years old.

▶▶ Extension

An additional problem is presented on Resource Sheet **c**.

To solve this children should be encouraged to draw on the strategy 'make an organised list'.

Solution: In 5 years, when Abigail is 12 and Peter is 24.

Unit **3** — *THE FOOTBALL LEAGUE*

▶ *Problem*

There are six teams in the football league.
Each team will play each of the other teams only once.
How many games will be played altogether?

NNS links

Solve mathematical problems or puzzles, recognise and explain patterns and relationships, generalise and predict. Suggest extensions by asking 'What if ...?

Express a relationship in words, orally and in writing.

Explain methods and reasoning about numbers, orally and in writing.

Problem-solving strategies

- ▓ Try a simpler case
- ▓ Draw a picture or diagram or make a model
- ▓ Make an organised list or table
- ▓ Look for a pattern

Overview

The problem encourages the children to use a systematic method of recording. This problem can be used to introduce the strategy 'try a simpler case'. The pattern of triangular numbers (+1 + 2 + 3 + ...) is also built up if the children use this strategy.

Resources

Lesson A
Interactive whiteboard
Can Do Problem-solving Year 5/P6 Whiteboard CD-ROM
Individual pupil whiteboards and pens
Counters

Lesson B
General Resource Sheet A and General Resource Sheet B – enlarged or copied onto OHT
Resource Sheet 3 Football League Table – one per pair
Individual pupil whiteboards and pens
Counters

Follow-up problems

Netball Practice
The Big Top

▶ *Introduction*

Begin by revising the problem-solving process. Click on the Five steps button to show this on the whiteboard screen.

Read and think

Show The Football League problem on the whiteboard. Give the children time to read the problem line by line. Ask the children to explain the problem to partners in their own words. Prompt for understanding:

What information are you given?

What information do you need in order solve the problem?

Ensure that the children are able to identify the key items of information in the problem.

SCREEN 1
Large notice board in a school hall with the problem displayed. Use this screen to set the context of the problem.

Choose a strategy

Allow time for the children to think independently and then ask them to discuss with a partner how they would each go about solving this problem.

Review the nine informal problem-solving strategies by clicking on the Strategies button on the screen:

Which strategies would be appropriate for solving this problem and which would not?

Allow a couple of minutes for children to discuss the range of suitable strategies with their partners. Prompt if necessary by encouraging the children to think about using a smaller number of teams.

How many games would two teams play? What about three teams?

Experiment

Use Screen 2 to work with a smaller number of teams.

Establish that if there were only one team in the league then no games would be played. Show on the whiteboard that if two teams played there would only be one game played. Allow the children time to experiment with three and four teams. Encourage them to make an organised list similar to the one on the whiteboard.

SCREEN 2
Use the drop down menu to select the number of teams to work with. Drag and drop teams to build up an organised list of fixtures for the number of teams selected.

continued

Consider

Ask the children how many matches would be played for three and four games in the league. Enter this into the table on Screen 3. Ask the children to continue for 5 and 6 teams.

SCREEN 3

Use the keypad or type the information for the number of games played into the table.

Report and record

Look back at the problem. Use Screen 3 to complete the table and move to the solution for 6 teams.

With 3 teams there would be 3 games.

15 games would be played if 6 teams were in the league.

Does this solution answer the question?

Ask the children to look at the table of results. Encourage them to look for a pattern. Can they explain how the pattern develops? The pattern is based on triangular numbers and can be calculated by adding consecutive numbers: + 1, + 2, + 3, + 4, + 5, etc. Can the children verbalise this?

Establish whether the children understand and can apply the 'try a simpler case' strategy and whether they can predict the next set of triangular numbers using the whiteboard diagram (Screen 3). The diagram in the solution box can be used to illustrate triangular numbers.

▶▶ *Extension*

EXTENSION SCREEN

This screen displays the data from Screen 3 and asks children to extend the problem.

Ask the children to predict the number of games that would be played. Ask them to explain why they have chosen that number.

Can they extend the pattern to 8, 9 and 10 teams?

▶▶ *Support*

● Work with the children to complete the table or diagram.

● Show the children how the pattern of triangular numbers develops by using counters or other concrete materials.

Solution

Main   15 games

Extension   For 7 teams, 21 games; for 8 teams, 28 games; for 9 teams, 36 games; for 10 teams, 45 games.

No. of teams	Games played
1	0
2	1
3	3
4	6
5	10
6	15

A table to record the number of games played if there was a certain number of teams in the league.

▶ *Introduction*

Begin by revising the problem-solving process. Display this by using an enlarged version of General Resource Sheet A or copying it onto OHT.

Read and think

Write The Football League problem on a flip chart. Give the children time to read the problem line by line. Ask each child to explain the problem to a partner in her/his own words. Prompt for understanding:

What information are you given?

What information do you need in order solve the problem?

Ensure that the children are able to identify the key items of information in the problem.

Choose a strategy

Display the nine problem-solving strategies by enlarging General Resource Sheet B.

Which strategies would be appropriate for solving this problem and which would not?

Allow a couple of minutes for children to discuss the range of suitable strategies with their partners. Prompt if necessary by encouraging the children to think about using a smaller number of teams, i.e. 'try a simpler case'. They should also suggest a method of recording, such as 'make an organised list or table'.

Experiment

Establish that if there was only one team in the league then no games would be played. Continue by showing that if two teams played there would be only one game played. Allow children time to work individually or in pairs to continue the process, moving to 3, 4, 5 and finally 6 teams. If required, Resource Sheet 3 can be used for the purpose.

Encourage the children to start recording the information as they work by using one of the following:

• an organised list   • a table   • a diagram.

Consider

Draw children together to review progress. If they have succeeded in working out the number of games for 6 teams, encourage the children to look for a pattern and try to predict the next number of the pattern that has evolved. Write the responses as to how the pattern is building up on the board or flip chart. Look for an explanation of the relationship between the numbers of teams and the numbers of games played. If desired, encourage the children to identify the (triangular) pattern the numbers would make if displayed as dots. Introduce the term 'triangular numbers'. If necessary, explain that triangular numbers can be arranged into a triangular pattern of dots. These are formed by + 1 + 2 + 3 + … and ask individual children to complete the pattern on the flip chart.

continued

Report and record

Look back at the problem.

With 2 teams there would be 1 game.

With 3 teams there would be 3 games (Team 1 v Team 2, Team 2 v Team 3, Team 1 v Team 3)

and so on.

15 games would be played if 6 teams were in the league.

Does this solution answer the question?

Record the solution on the board or flip chart. Establish whether individual children can explain the pattern of triangular numbers.

▶▶ Extension

Ask the children to work out the number of games for a league with 7, 8, 9, 10 teams in it.

▶▶ Support

● Work with the children to complete the table or diagram.

● Show the children how the pattern of triangular numbers develops by using counters or other concrete materials.

Solution

Main 15 games

Extension For 7 teams, 21 games; for 8 teams, 28 games; for 9 teams, 36 games; for 10 teams, 45 games.

No. of teams	Games played
1	0
2	1
3	3
4	6
5	10
6	15

A table to record the number of games played if there was a certain number of teams in the league.

▶ **Problem**

The netball team are practising their passing.
The seven players are standing in a circle.
Every member of the team has to pass the ball to every other player.
How many passes are made altogether?

NNS links

Solve mathematical problems or puzzles; recognise and explain patterns and relationships; generalise and predict. Suggest extensions by asking 'What if …?'

Express a relationship in words, orally and in writing.

Problem-solving strategies

▪ Try a simpler case

▪ Look for a pattern

▪ Make an organised list or table

Overview

The problem reinforces the strategies that the children met in The Football League. A variety of strategies can be used. As there are a large number of players, some children may begin by using 'try a simpler case'. Draw the children together to establish progress being made as the problem is being solved. At this point some children may have moved on to organising the data in a table. Suggest this as the most effective strategy at this point. The extension moves the children onto identifying the pattern and writing about it. The pattern that emerges could be discussed in a plenary session.

Three differentiated resource sheets are provided on the *Resources CD-ROM*. These can be used to support this activity.

▷▷ **Core**

Resource Sheet **a** presents the problem.

Solution:

No of players	No of passes
2	2
3	6
4	12
5	20
6	30
7	42

For seven players there would be 42 passes.

▷▷ **Support**

Resource Sheet **b** helps the children to put the strategy 'try a simpler case' into practice by taking them through the number of passes for 3, 4 and 5 players. Children could be prompted to draw a table to complete the sequence for 6 and 7 players.

▷▷ **Extension**

Resource Sheet **c** asks the children to write the pattern and make the generalisation in words.

Solution: Multiply the number of players by one less than itself.

▶ Problem

The Big Top has eight sides.
There is a pole at each corner and a large pole in the middle.
To make sure it doesn't fall down, every corner pole is connected to the middle pole.
and to the poles on either side of it by a rope.
How many ropes are there holding the Big Top up?

NNS links

Solve mathematical problems or puzzles, recognise and explain patterns and relationships, generalise and predict. Suggest extensions by asking 'What if ...?'

Express a relationship in words, orally and in writing.

Problem-solving strategies

- Try a simpler case
- Draw a picture or diagram or make a model
- Look for a pattern
- Make an organised list or table

Overview

The problem reinforces the strategies that the children met in The Football League and Netball Practice. A variety of strategies can be used. Some children may use 'try a simpler case' while others may draw a diagram. If the strategy 'try a simpler case' is used children can start to work with a three-sided and then a four-sided shape. Attention could be drawn to the pattern emerging. At this point some children may have moved on to organising the data in a table. Suggest this as an effective strategy at this point. The extension asks the children to write about the pattern they have identified and asks them to work out how many ropes there would be if the Big Top has 12 sides.

Three differentiated resource sheets are provided on the *Resources CD-ROM*. These can be used to support this activity.

▶▶ Core

Resource Sheet **a** presents the problem.
Solution: For a big top with 8 sides there would be 16 ropes.

▶▶ Support

Resource Sheet **b** helps the children to put the strategy 'try a simpler case' into practice by taking them through the number of ropes for a 3, 4 and 5-sided shape. Children could be prompted to draw a table to complete the sequence up to 8 sides.

Sides	3	4	5	6	7	8
Ropes	6	8	10	12	14	16

▶▶ Extension

Resource Sheet **c** asks the children to write the pattern and make the generalisation in words.

In a plenary session this could be developed further by asking: *What if the Big Top had 12 sides? How many ropes would there be then?*
Solution: 24

Unit 4 ALIENS

▶ *Problem*

Ben is making Aliens using his model kit.
There are: 2 types of head
2 types of body
2 types of feet
How many different Aliens can he make using all the possible combinations of head, body and feet?

NNS links

Solve mathematical problems or puzzles, recognise and explain patterns and relationships, generalise and predict. Suggest extensions by asking 'What if …?

Explain methods and reasoning about numbers, orally and in writing.

Problem-solving strategies

- ▨ Make an organised list or table
- ▨ Draw a picture or diagram or make a model

Overview

This is a problem-solving activity that involves the children in identifying all the different combinations that can be made from a given number of variables. The main strategy used is to 'make an organised list or table'. The extension activity involves increasing the number of variables with the possibility of identifying the rule involved.

Resources

Lesson A
Interactive whiteboard
Can Do Problem-solving Year 5/P6 Whiteboard CD-ROM
Individual pupil whiteboards and pens

Lesson B
General Resource Sheet A and General Resource Sheet B – enlarged or copied onto OHT
Resource Sheet 4 Aliens – copy and cut out for each pair
Individual pupil whiteboards (or paper) and pens

Follow-up problems

Ice Creams
The Chime Bars

· ·

▶ *Introduction*

Begin by revising the problem-solving process. Click on the Five steps button to show this on the whiteboard screen.

Read and think

Show the Aliens problem on the whiteboard. Prompt for understanding:

What information are you given?

What information do you require to solve the problem?

SCREEN 1
Show the problem on the whiteboard. The problem appears in words after a short animation. This screen sets the context and text for the problem.

Allow time for the children to think independently first and then ask them to discuss with a partner how they would go about solving the problem.

Choose a strategy

Revise the nine problem-solving strategies by clicking on the Strategies button on the screen.

Which strategies would be appropriate for this problem and which would not?

Appropriate strategies offered should include 'make an organised list or table' or 'draw a picture or diagram'.

Discuss using these strategies to solve the problem.

Experiment

Use Screen 2 to demonstrate one possible combination of head, body and feet. The Aliens that have been made are shown at the top of the screen.

SCREEN 2
Drag and drop the body parts into the box to make an Alien. Click on the Check alien button to transfer it to the panel at the top.

Allow the children, in pairs or small groups, to click and drag until they have all the possible combinations. The number of Aliens made is recorded.

continued

Consider

Ask children:

How do you know that you have found all the possible combinations?

Establish the need to produce an organised list or table.

SCREEN 3
Drag and drop the labelled body parts to the table.

Screen 3 shows graphics of Alien parts, this time with a number beside each one.

Ask children to enter the possible combinations into the grid, working systematically, first on paper, then in pairs or groups on the whiteboard',

e.g. 1 1 1

     1 2 1 etc.

Report and record

Look carefully at the table created on the whiteboard to record the combinations.

Can you see the pattern that could be used as a checking strategy to find out whether all the combinations have been found?

SOLUTION SCREEN
This runs an animation showing the table from Screen 3 being filled in. All possible combinations are also shown.

Head, body and feet for each type are used the same number of times. All head type 1 aliens have a reflective partner with head type 2 aliens. Give the children time to reflect and evaluate their strategies with their partners.

If they were to solve a similar problem in the future how would they adapt their strategies?

Can you see any relationship between the number of each body part that you started with and the solution?

▶▶ *Extension*

EXTENSION SCREEN
This provides another head. The children can repeat the process as in Screen 3.

How would you approach the problem if an additional element was introduced?

Encourage the children to record systematically. Invite individuals to come to the whiteboard to complete the table.

▶▶ *Support*

● Support the children with their preferred strategy or introduce new ones – for example, asking the children to draw pictures of each combination before moving to the whiteboard activity.

Solution

See also the Solution screen.

Main   There are eight possible combinations:

Head	Body	Feet
1	1	1
1	1	2
1	2	2
1	2	1
2	2	2
2	1	1
2	2	1
2	1	2

Extension   There are 12 possible combinations.

▶ *Introduction*

Begin by revising the problem-solving process. Display this by using an enlarged version of General Resource Sheet A or copying it onto OHT.

Read and think

Write the Aliens problem on a flip chart. Prompt for understanding:

What information are you given?

What information do you require to solve the problem?

Allow time for the children to think independently first and then ask them to discuss with a partner how they would go about solving the problem.

Choose a strategy

Display the nine problem-solving strategies by enlarging General Resource Sheet B or copying it onto OHT. Ask the children how they would attempt to solve the problem.

Allow the children time to think independently first and then ask them to discuss with a partner how they would go about solving the problem. Appropriate strategies offered should include 'make an organised list' or 'draw a picture or diagram or make a model'.

Discuss using these strategies to solve the problem.

Experiment

Circulate a full set of body parts from Resource Sheet 4 to each pair or small group. Demonstrate one possible combination of head and body by attaching one combination of head, body and feet to a flip chart. Ensure that this is then removed so that no repetition of this arrangement can be made at this stage.

Allow the children, in pairs or small groups, to make their own combinations using the prepared body parts or by asking them to draw them.

- Head 1
- Body 1
- Feet 1

Create a tally on a flip chart to count up the number of combinations that are being made. Encourage the children to keep one element constant.

continued

Consider

How do you know that you have found all the possible combinations?

Establish the need to produce an organised list or table (see example, below).

Prepare a list of the alien body parts on the flip chart, this time with a number beside each one. Ask the children to enter all the possible combinations into the grid, working systematically first on paper, then in pairs or groups on the board or flip chart.

Allow the children time to complete their lists or tables if necessary.

Report and record

Look carefully at the table created to record the combinations.

Can you see the pattern that could be used as a checking strategy to find out whether all the combinations have been found?

Head, body and feet for each type are used the same number of times. All head type 1 aliens have a reflective partner with head type 2 aliens. Give the children time to reflect and evaluate their strategies with their partner.

If you were to solve a similar problem in the future how would you adapt your strategies?

Can you see any relationship between the number of each body part that you started with and the solution?

▶▶ **Extension**

A further problem could be provided:

There is now another type of head. How many combinations of Aliens can you make using all types of head, body and feet?

▶▶ **Support**

● Support the children with their preferred strategy or introduce new ones – for example, asking the children to draw pictures of each combination.

Solution

See also the Solution screen.

Main There are eight possible combinations:

Head	Body	Feet
1	1	1
1	1	2
1	2	2
1	2	1
2	2	2
2	1	1
2	2	1
2	1	2

Extension There are 12 possible combinations.

▶ *Problem*

An ice cream shop sells three flavours of ice cream: strawberry, chocolate and vanilla. How many combinations of triple-scoop cones can the shop sell using the three flavours?

| NNS links | Solve mathematical problems or puzzles, recognise and explain patterns and relationships, generalise and predict. Suggest extensions by asking 'What if ...?' |

| Problem-solving strategies | ▪ Make an organised list or table
▪ Reason logically |

| Overview | The problem asks the children to consider all the combinations that can be made. The two key strategies here are to organise the combinations into an organised list and to work through the combinations in a systematic way. Children should not forget the combinations of all one flavour. Colour coding could help with recording the data as could representing the flavours by using a letter. |

Three differentiated resource sheets are provided on the *Resources CD-ROM*. These can be used to support this activity.

▸▸ Core

Resource Sheet **a** presents the problem.

Solution: 10 different combinations.

CCC	VVV	SSS	SSV	SSC
VVC	SVC	CCS	VVS	CCV

▸▸ Support

On Resource Sheet **b** the problem is simplified and uses only two flavours. The shop sells both single and double scoops so the children should consider single as well as the combinations of doubles. Care should be taken not to record combinations twice, e.g. CV and VC.

Solution: 9 combinations.

S	V	C	SS	VV	CC	SV	SC	VC

▸▸ Extension

On Resource Sheet **c** a different problem is presented, which will involve children in using the same problem-solving strategies as the core problem.

Would you expect the same solution as the first problem?

Can you explain why you get a different solution?

Solution: 27

111	211	311
112	212	312
113	213	313
121	221	321
122	222	322
123	223	323
131	231	331
132	232	332
133	233	333

Unit 4

▶ *Problem*

The music group has three chime bars E, G, B.
List all the three-note tunes that can be played using these chime bars.

NNS links

Solve mathematical problems or puzzles, recognise and explain patterns and relationships, generalise and predict. Suggest extensions by asking 'What if …?'

Problem-solving strategies

- Make an organised list or table
- Reason logically

Overview

This problem utilises the strategies used in other problems in this unit. If children have already done the activity in Ice Creams they will recognise the type of systematic listing that is required for this problem. In the plenary session demonstrate a systematic listing if no one has shown evidence of such, and emphasise its efficiency in minimising omissions.

Different types of listings could be discussed.

Three differentiated resource sheets are provided on the *Resources CD-ROM*. These can be used to support this activity.

▶▶ *Core*

Resource Sheet **a** presents the main problem.

Solution: 27 combinations.

EEE	EEG	EEB	EGG	EBB	EGB	EBG	EGE	EBE
GGG	GEE	GBB	GEB	GBE	GCE	GGB	GBG	GEG
BBB	BGG	BEE	BGE	BGB	BEG	BEB	BBG	BBE

▶▶ *Support*

The problem on Resource Sheet **b** offers a simplified version and uses only combinations of two notes. Encourage the children to organise the combinations into an organised list in the same way as they would for the main problem.

Solution: 9 combinations

AA, AB, BA, BB, CC, AC, BC, CA, CB.

▶▶ *Extension*

The problem is extended on Resource Sheet **c** by asking how many possibilities there are including two-note combinations.

Solution: 36

The full list is as for the main problem plus

EE, EG, EB, GG, GB, GE, BB, BE, BG.

▶ Problem

Craig has gone to play at his friend Peter's house.
The two boys are playing a game. Peter is trying to guess Craig's telephone number from the clues Craig gives him.
The telephone number is four digits in length.
Can you work out the number?

Clue 1: All digits added together total 21.
Clue 2: The middle two digits are the same.
Clue 3: If you multiply the middle digits you get the last one.

NNS links

Solve mathematical problems or puzzles, recognise and explain patterns and relationships, generalise and predict. Suggest extensions by asking 'What if …?'

Use all four operations to solve word problems involving numbers in 'real life'.

Explain methods and reasoning about numbers, orally and in writing.

Problem-solving strategies

▪ Trial and improvement
▪ Reason logically

Overview

This problem gives the children further practice in using the strategy of 'trial and improvement'. The children are encouraged to make an approximate or rough calculation and then to improve upon it as they think about the calculations required to solve it. The clues are presented one by one in the activity.

Resources

Lesson A
Interactive whiteboard
Can Do Problem-solving Year 5/P6 Whiteboard CD-ROM
Individual pupil whiteboards and pens

Lesson B
General Resource Sheet A and General Resource Sheet B – enlarged or copied on OHT
Resource Sheet 5 Craig's Telephone Number – one per child
Resource Sheet 6 Peter's Telephone Number
Individual pupil whiteboards and pens

Follow-up problems

PIN Number
Number Puzzles

▶ *Introduction*

Begin by revising the problem-solving process. Click on the Five steps button to show this on the whiteboard screen.

Read and think

Show Craig's Telephone Number problem on the whiteboard. Ask the children to read the problem together.

What information are you given? Is there enough information?

SCREEN 1
The problem is presented.

What information do you need to solve the problem?

Explain that the children will be given the clues one by one.

Choose a strategy

Revise the nine problem-solving strategies by clicking on the Strategies button on the whiteboard screen.

Which strategies would be appropriate for this problem and which would not?

Allow a couple of minutes for children to discuss the range of suitable strategies with their partners. Appropriate strategies offered should include 'trial and improvement'.

Experiment

Encourage the children to think about the phone number they are trying to make and about the calculations that are required to find each digit. Ask them to decide if each number is 'reasonable'. Prompt for each clue if necessary, e.g.:

SCREENS 2/3/4
Drag and drop digits into the empty boxes.

Clue 1

The digits involved must be quite small as added together the four digits add up to only 21.

Clue 3

The fourth number must be a square number as the two middle numbers are the same and when multiplied together will provide this digit.

Ask them to work on paper initially and then to test their answers on the whiteboard screen.

Consider

If necessary, prompt the children to use a systematic approach in finding a solution – for example:

Use one piece of information in the problem and see what effect it has.

When the children have a solution, ask them in pairs to check for further possibilities and to explain the reasons why there is only one possible solution to this problem.

Press Done to activate the Solution screen.

continued

> Report and record

Look back to the problem. Ask for a solution to the original problem.

Does this solution answer the question?

Show the solution on the whiteboard.

> **SOLUTION SCREEN**
> This shows the correct telephone number and the clues.

Ask the children to offer their explanations as to why there is only one solution to this problem. The determining factor is that the digits must add up to 21.

Allow the children the opportunity to evaluate the strategy used.

How would you adapt your strategies if you were to solve similar problems in the future?

>> *Extension*

> **EXTENSION SCREEN**
> This shows the extension problem. Drag and drop the digit cards into empty boxes.

Use the extension problem on the whiteboard. Children could work in pairs before coming to the whiteboard to show their solutions. Alternatively this could be done as a class activity. You might also extend the problem in different ways. For example, identify clues for a five-digit telephone number. You might also extend the range of maths involved, e.g. 'the middle number is three-quarters of the two outside numbers'. Children could also write their own problem.

>> *Support*

● Support the children in identifying the required calculations and in recording the stages of the problem.

Solution

See also the Solution screen.

Main	6339
Extension	3945 and 2606

Unit 5 — LESSON B

▶ *Introduction*

Begin by revising the problem-solving process. Display this by using an enlarged version of General Resource Sheet A.

Read and think

Write Craig's Telephone Number problem on a flip chart.

Ask the children to read the problem together.

What information are you given?

What information do you need to solve the problem?

Ensure that the children are able to identify the key items of information in the problem.

Choose a strategy

Display the nine problem-solving strategies by enlarging General Resource Sheet B or copying it onto OHT.

Which strategies would be appropriate for this problem and which would not?

Give each child a copy of Resource Sheet 5. Allow a couple of minutes for children to discuss the range of suitable strategies with their partners. Appropriate strategies offered should include 'trial and improvement'.

Experiment

Encourage the children to think about the phone number they are trying to make and about the calculations that are required to find each digit. Ask them to decide if each number is 'reasonable'. Prompt for each clue if necessary, e.g.:

Clue 1

The digits involved must be quite small as added together the four digits add up to only 21.

Clue 3

The fourth number must be a square number as the two middle numbers are the same and when multiplied together will provide this digit.

Ask them to show their workings out on Resource Sheet 5 in addition to filling in the answer box on the sheet.

Consider

If necessary, prompt the children to use a systematic approach in finding a solution – for example:

Use one piece of information in the problem and see what effect it has.

When the children have a solution, ask them in pairs to check for further possibilities and to explain the reasons why there is only one possible solution to this problem.

continued

Report and record

Look back to the problem. Ask for a solution to the original problem.

Does this solution answer the question?

Record the solution on the flip chart.

Ask the children to offer their explanations as to why there is only one solution to this problem. The determining factor is that the digits must add up to 21.

Record an explanation on the whiteboard on which all the children agree.

Allow the children the opportunity to evaluate the strategy used.

How would you adapt your strategies if you were to solve similar problems in the future?

⯈ Extension

An additional problem is presented on Resource Sheet 6. You might also extend the problem in different ways. For example, identify clues for a five-digit telephone number. You might also extend the range of maths involved, e.g. 'the middle number is three-quarters of the two outside numbers'.

⯈ Support

● Support the children in identifying the required calculations and in recording the stages of the problem.

Solution

Main	6339
Extension	3945 and 2606

▶ Problem

Marie has just opened a bank account.
She has been given a cash card and a four-digit PIN number so that she can take money from her account using a cash machine.
She says that the middle two digits when multiplied together make an odd number more than 21 but less than 30.
If you subtract the second digit from the third digit you get the last digit.
All four digits added together total 20.
What is Marie's PIN number?

NNS links

Use all four operations to solve word problems involving numbers in 'real life'.

Solve mathematical problems or puzzles, recognise and explain patterns and relationships, generalise and predict. Suggest extensions by asking 'What if …?'

Explain methods and reasoning about numbers, orally and in writing.

Problem-solving strategies

■ Trial and improvement

■ Reason logically

Overview

The problem gives the opportunity to use all four operations in the context of finding a PIN number. The problem will give children the opportunity to refine skills in trial and improvement. It builds on the skills used in Craig's Telephone Number. Children should be encouraged to use a combination of mental methods and jottings to record the stages of their calculations. They could also be asked to explain how they reached the answer during the plenary session.

Three differentiated resource sheets are provided on the *Resources CD-ROM*. These can be used to support this activity.

▶▶ Core

Resource Sheet **a** presents the main problem.
Solution: 2396

▶▶ Support

A simplified problem is presented on Resource Sheet **b**.
Solution: 4784

▶▶ Extension

After completing the main problem, on Resource Sheet **c** children can create their own four-digit PIN numbers with instructions. In addition to the four operations children could introduce more varied vocabulary, e.g. a factor of, is a square number, is an eighth of, etc. Problems can be exchanged and solved. Alternatively Resource Sheet **c** can be used as a whole-class activity in the plenary session.
Solution: 2396

▶ **Problem**

The problems are all number puzzles and are shown on the resource sheets.

(**NNS links**)

Solve mathematical problems or puzzles, recognise and explain patterns and relationships, generalise and predict. Suggest extensions by asking 'What if …?'

Choose and use appropriate number operations and appropriate ways of calculating to solve problems.

Explain methods and reasoning about numbers, orally and in writing.

(**Problem-solving strategies**)

▓ Trial and improvement

(**Overview**)

There are three problems provided giving the opportunity to use all four operations. Each problem will give children the opportunity to refine skills in trial and improvement and build on the skills used in Craig's Telephone Number. Children should be encouraged to use a combination of mental methods and jottings to record the stages of their calculations. Some specific mathematical vocabulary is used in the problems. This should be revised before the children attempt the problems.

Three differentiated resource sheets are provided on the *Resources CD-ROM*. These can be used to support this activity.

Unit 5

continued

▶▶ Core

Resource Sheet **a** presents three problems. Ensure that children understand the meaning of 'consecutive' and 'product' before they begin the problems. Draw the children together during the process to establish progress being made as the problems are being solved. This will give the children the opportunity to share strategies and evaluate the strategies they are using. Once the problem has been solved ask the children individually or in pairs to explain their reasoning.

Solution: a) 13 × 14   b) 4, 6, 7
c)   or 3, 7, 8

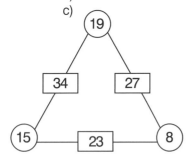

▶▶ Support

A different set of three problems is presented on Resource Sheet **b**. These are easier than those in the core activity. Ensure that children know the meaning of 'sum' and 'difference' before they attempt the problems.

Solution: a) 13 × 6   b) 16 and 17; or
c)   15 and 18; or 14
                                          and 19, etc

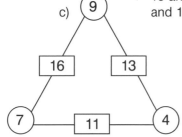

▶▶ Extension

Resource Sheet **c** presents problems that are designed to be more challenging. Ensure that the children know the meaning of the terms 'product', 'consecutive' and 'difference' before starting work. For Problems a) and b) a calculator could be used to speed the process of calculation.

Solution: a) 97 × 84 = 8148   b) 14, 12
c)

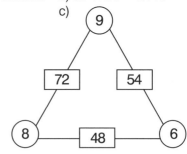

42

▶ *Problem*

The treasure chest holds a candlestick, a gold bar, a statue, a crown and a bag of silver coins. Indiana Smith can only carry 9 kilograms in his rucksack. He wants to take treasure of the largest possible value. Any number of items can be taken but the total weight cannot be more than 9 kilograms. Work out the items that he should take.

ITEM	Candlestick	Gold bar	Statue	Crown	Bag of silver coins
WEIGHT (kg)	4	8	6	2	3
VALUE (£)	30	120	90	50	20

NNS links

Use all four operations to solve word problems involving numbers in 'real life'.

Explain methods and reasoning about numbers, orally and in writing.

Problem-solving strategies

▓ Trial and improvement

▓ Reason logically

Overview

This problem gives the children further practice and reinforcement in using the strategy 'trial and improvement'. The children are encouraged to try a variety of different approaches such as 'trial and improvement' or 'act out the situation'. If they are able to justify and explain why one strategy is more efficient than the other, then this will reinforce the skill 'consider a better solution'. The extension activity further develops this approach.

Resources

Lesson A
Interactive whiteboard
Can Do Problem-solving Year 5/P6 Whiteboard CD-ROM
Resource Sheet 7 The Rucksack – copy and cut out one per group (optional)
Individual pupil whiteboards and pens

Lesson B
General Resource Sheet A and General Resource Sheet B – enlarged or copied onto OHT
Resource Sheet 7 The Rucksack – copy and cut out one per group
Individual pupil whiteboards and pens

Follow-up problems

The Computer Game
The Long Jump

▶ *Introduction*

Begin by revising the problem-solving process. Click on the Five steps button to show this on the whiteboard screen.

Read and think

SCREEN 1
The problem is presented on screen.

Show The Rucksack problem on the whiteboard. Ask the children to read the problem together.

What information are you given?

What information do you need to solve the problem?

The children should realise that they need both the weight and the value of the objects to work out the solution.

Choose a strategy

SCREEN 2
Drag and drop each item into the table to reveal the weight and value.

Revise the nine problem-solving strategies by clicking on the Strategies button on the whiteboard screen.

Which strategies would be appropriate for this problem and which would not?

Allow a couple of minutes for children to discuss the range of suitable strategies with their partners. Appropriate strategies offered might include 'act out the situation', 'trial and improvement' or 'reason logically'. Drag and drop each item into the table and discuss how they would begin to solve the problem.

Experiment

SCREEN 3
Drag and drop the chosen items into the rucksack. Click on Done.

Move to Screen 3. Show the table on the screen with the weights and value of the treasure.

Ask the children to look at the weight allowance and work out the combinations of items and prices. Ask the children to work in pairs to try to solve the problem.

The pairs should work on paper first and then on the whiteboard to test out their ideas.

Copy and cut out sets of items and labels from Resource Sheet 7 to help the children with their experimentation.

Consider

Encourage the children to look at 'value for money' when deciding whether to include an item in the rucksack. Emphasise the need to work systematically through the problem. Click on Done to activate the Solution screen.

continued

Look back to the problem.

Ask for a solution to the original problem.

Does the solution answer the question?

Move to the Solution screen.

Report and record

SOLUTION SCREEN
This shows the correct items in the rucksack: the crown and the statue.

Take oral explanations from the children on how they arrived at the solution. Be careful not to lead the children to the conclusion that there is only one correct way to tackle this problem.

Allow the children time to evaluate the methods they used to solve the problem.

If you were to solve a similar problem in the future how would you adapt or refine the strategies you have used?

▶▶ *Extension*

EXTENSION SCREEN
Click and drag the chosen items into the rucksack as in Screen 3.

The maximum weight is changed to 12 kg. Allow the children to experiment on paper before trying their solutions on the whiteboard. Alternatively, this could be done as a whole-class activity.

▶▶ *Support*

● Give support to the children to 'act out the situation', using the items on Resource Sheet 7 or other representations of the treasure.

Solution

See also the Solution screen.

Main   The statue and the crown: weight 8 kg, value £140.

Extension   Candlestick, statue and crown: weight 12 kg, value £170
                Gold bar and crown: weight 10 kg, value £170

▶ Introduction

Begin by revising the problem-solving process. Display this by using an enlarged version of General Resource Sheet A or copying it onto OHT.

Read and think

Write The Rucksack problem on a flip chart. Ask the children to read the problem together.

What information are you given?

What information do you need to solve the problem?

Ensure that the children are able to identify the key items of information in the problem.

Choose a strategy

Revise the nine problem-solving strategies by enlarging General Resource Sheet B or copying it onto OHT.

Which strategies would be appropriate for this problem and which would not?

Allow a couple of minutes for children to discuss the range of suitable strategies with their partners. Appropriate strategies offered might include 'act out the situation', 'trial and improvement' or 'reason logically'. Discuss each strategy in turn and ask the children how they would use it to solve the problem.

Experiment

Write the table below on the flip chart:

ITEM	Candlestick	Gold bar	Statue	Crown	Bag of silver coins
WEIGHT (kg)	4	8	6	2	3
VALUE (£)	30	120	90	50	20

Ask the children to look at the weight allowance and work out the combinations of items and prices. Ask the children to work in pairs to try to solve the problem.

The pairs should work on paper first, using a combination of mental methods and jottings. They could use the sets of items and labels from Resource Sheet 7 to help with their experimentation.

Consider

Draw the children together to discuss progress. Encourage them to look at 'value for money' when deciding whether to include an item in the rucksack. For example, the candlestick weighs 4 kg but is only worth £30 – each kilogram is worth less than £10 – but the gold bar weighs 8 kg and is worth £120 – each kilogram is worth more than £10.

Emphasise the need to work systematically through the problem.

Report and record

Look back to the problem.

Ask for a solution to the original problem.

Does the solution answer the question?

Record the solution on the whiteboard.

Take oral explanations from the children on how they arrived at the solution. Be careful not to lead the children to the conclusion that there is only one correct way to tackle this problem.

Allow the children time to evaluate the methods they used to solve the problem.

If you were to solve a similar problem in the future how would you adapt or refine the strategies you have used?

▶▶ Extension

Extend this problem by introducing a 'What if ...?'

What if Indiana Smith could carry 12 kg in his rucksack? Which items should he choose?

▶▶ Support

● Give support to the children to 'act out the situation', using the items on Resource Sheet 7 or other representations of the treasure.

Solution

Main	The statue and the crown: weight 8 kg, value £140
Extension	Candlestick, statue and crown: weight 12 kg, value £170
	Gold bar and crown: weight 10 kg, value £170

▶ **Problem**

Miss Khan has a new computer game which can be played by two or three players at a time.

She wants everyone to have a turn.

The game takes 20 minutes with 2 people playing or 35 minutes with 3 people playing.

There are 31 pupils in the class and only one computer.

Miss Khan wants to take the shortest possible time and give everyone a turn.

How should she organise the players into groups?

NNS links

Use all four operations to solve word problems involving time.

Problem-solving strategies

- Trial and improvement
- Reason logically

Overview

To solve this problem the children will need look carefully at the question they are asked. Once the strategy has been chosen the children must identify the starting point. There are two elements that need to be considered: the number in the groups and the time it takes the groups to play. Encourage the children to consider similar problems they have solved and strategies they have used in order to solve them. Draw the children together to establish progress being made as the problem is being solved. This will give the children the opportunity to share strategies and evaluate the strategies they are using.

Three differentiated resource sheets are provided on the *Resources CD-ROM*. These can be used to support this activity.

▶▶ **Core**

Resource Sheet **a** presents the main problem for the children to solve.

Solution: The shortest time is 315 minutes (14 groups of 2 and 1 group of 3).

▶▶ **Support**

Resource Sheet **b** contains a simpler version of the problem. Some additional support with identifying the different elements in the problem may be appropriate for some children.

Solution: The shortest time is 200 minutes for 10 groups of 3 people.

▶▶ **Extension**

On Resource Sheet **c** the children are asked to complete the main problem and then asked: 'What if two more pupils joined the class? How should Miss Khan organise the class now?'

Solution: 15 groups of 2 and 1 group of 3 = 335 minutes.

Unit **6** FOLLOW-UP PROBLEM: THE LONG JUMP

▶ *Problem*

The Elmhill District School Sports Day has team events.
In the long jump five children take part and the three best jumps count for the total distance jumped.
Which school won the Long Jump Competition?

School	Jump 1	Jump 2	Jump 3	Jump 4	Jump 5
Lea Road	2·9 m	1·6 m	2·15 m	2·6 m	2·45 m
Elm Street	2·05 m	1·7 m	1·65 m	2·3 m	2·4 m

NNS links — Use all four operations to solve word problems involving length.

Problem-solving strategies — ■ Reason logically

Overview

This problem is a multi-stage problem and children will need to read it carefully in order to decide the starting point. There are three elements that need to be considered. First, children should decide which jumps should be used, then total them and finally compare the two totals to determine the winning team. This will give the children the opportunity to share strategies and evaluate their own strategies.

Three differentiated resource sheets are provided on the *Resources CD-ROM*. These can be used to support this activity.

 Core

Resource Sheet **a** presents the main problem for the children to solve.

Solution: The three best jumps for Lea Road total 7·95 m and for Elm Street 6·75 m; therefore Lea Road won the competition.

▶▶ *Support*

Resource Sheet **b** is a simpler version of the problem, which contains decimals to one place only. Some additional support with identifying the different elements in the problem may be appropriate for some children.

Solution: The three best jumps for Lea Road total 7·5 m and for Elm Street 6·6 m; therefore Lea Road won the competition.

▶▶ *Extension*

On Resource Sheet **c** the children are asked to look at the results to answer three questions.

Solution: a) See Core solution. b) The difference between the longest and shortest jumps for each school is Lea Road 1·3 m, Elm Street 0·75 m. c) If all five jumps had counted Lea Road would have won.

Unit 7 THE AIRPORT

▶ *Problem*

The airport bus leaves every 10 minutes.
A helicopter takes off every 15 minutes.
A passenger aircraft takes off every 6 minutes.
If they all started operating at 8 a.m. when would be the next time that they all set off together?

NNS links

Solve mathematical problems or puzzles, recognise and explain patterns and relationships, generalise and predict. Suggest extensions by asking 'What if …?'

Problem-solving strategies

■ Reason logically

■ Trial and improvement

■ Make an organised list or table

Overview

This problem extends the children's ability to produce an organised list or table and reason logically. They will also learn how to develop an organised, systematic and experimental approach in the implementation of these strategies.

Resources

Lesson A
Interactive whiteboard
Can Do Problem-solving Year 5/P6 Whiteboard CD-ROM
Resource Sheet 8 Timeline – one per child
Individual pupil whiteboards (or paper) and pens

Lesson B
General Resource Sheet A and General Resource Sheet B – enlarged or copied onto OHT
Resource Sheet 8 Timeline – one per child
Individual pupil whiteboards (or paper) and pens

Follow-up problems

Old Macdonald
The Bus Station

▶ **Introduction**

Begin by revising the problem-solving process. Click on the Five steps button to show this on the whiteboard screen.

Read and think

SCREEN 1
The problem appears on screen. Press Play to activate a short animation which sets the context for the problem.

Show The Airport problem on the whiteboard. Give the children time to read the problem line by line. Ask the children to read the problem together.

What information are you given?

What information do you need to solve the problem?

Ensure that the children are able to identify the key items of information in the problem.

Choose a strategy

Revise the nine problem-solving strategies by clicking on the Strategies button on the whiteboard screen.

Which strategies would be appropriate for this problem and which would not?

Allow a couple of minutes for children to discuss the range of suitable strategies with their partners. Appropriate strategies offered should include 'make an organised list or table', 'trial and improvement' and 'reason logically'. Discuss using these strategies to solve the problem.

Experiment

SCREEN 2
Click on the timeline to plot the departure times for the plane, bus and helicopter.

Discuss producing an organised list to work out the departure times. Children will have had experience of this previously.

The whiteboard activity suggests using a timeline, though a simple table or list would also be appropriate.

What do we need to find out from the timelines? (Record when the three times coincide.)

At what time would the first aircraft take off?

Ask an individual to come to the whiteboard and mark the time on the timeline.

Ask the children to attempt the problem on paper, and to discuss the problem with a partner and the methods of recording it.

continued

Consider

Allow individuals to come to the whiteboard to record their times and watch for anyone who shows evidence of using multiples or factors in their work. Draw attention to this if appropriate to predict a pattern that may emerge because of the numbers that are being used. The numbers are factors of 30, therefore all three will take off together after 30 minutes.

Emphasise that in order to solve the problem they need to adopt a systematic approach.

How did your table/list help you to solve the problem?

Press Done to activate the Solution screen.

Report and record

At what time did a bus, a helicopter and an aircraft set off together?

Read the problem again. Take feedback from the class. Show the solution on the Solution screen, referring to the links between them, i.e. the time differences are all factors of 30.

SOLUTION SCREEN
This shows the time that they all depart together. Press Play to show the animation.

If you were to solve a similar problem in the future how would you adapt your strategies?

Would you use anyone else's strategy or approach in organising information?

▶▶ Extension

EXTENSION SCREEN
Introduce the extension problem. Click on the timeline to plot the times as in Screen 2.

The extension problem asks children to work out the next time they all leave together. Allow the children to work on this in pairs or alternatively it can be used as a whole-class activity.

▶▶ Support

● Supply children with copies of an empty timeline, which is provided on Resource Sheet 8. Help them begin to draw a simple table or list format to record their work.

Solution

See also the Solution screen.

Main	8.30 a.m.
Extension	9.00 a.m.

▶ Introduction

Begin by revising the problem-solving process. Display this by using an enlarged version of General Resource Sheet A.

Read and think

Write The Airport problem on a flip chart. Ask the children to read the problem together.

What information are you given?

What information do you need to solve the problem?

Ensure that the children are able to identify the key items of information in the problem.

Choose a strategy

Revise the nine problem-solving strategies by referring to the strategies on General Resource Sheet B.

Which strategies would be appropriate for this problem and which would not?

Allow a couple of minutes for children to discuss the range of suitable strategies with their partners. Appropriate strategies offered should include 'make an organised list or table', 'trial and improvement' and 'reason logically'. Discuss using these strategies to solve the problem.

Experiment

Allow children time either individually or in groups to experiment with devising a list or table to record the times that the different forms of transport leave the airport. This can be either in a table or simple list. Some children may decide to work with a timeline, marking off the times. Using this method they will very quickly see the common departure time.

Consider

Draw the children together to discuss methods being used. Emphasise that in order to solve the problem they need to adopt a systematic approach.

If appropriate, encourage the children to predict a pattern that may emerge because of the numbers that are being used. The numbers are factors of 30, therefore all three will leave together after 30 minutes.

Report and record

At what time did a bus, helicopter and aircraft set off together?

Read the problem again. Take feedback from the class. Ask children:

How did you organise your information. Which listing did you begin with and why?

If you were to solve a similar problem in the future how would you adapt your strategies?

Would you use anyone else's strategy or approach in organising information?

▶▶ Extension

An extension to the problem is provided as a 'What if…?' question.

Introduce the baggage car, which leaves every 12 minutes.

If they all started at 8 a.m. what would be the next time that they all set off together?

Allow children to solve this independently or discuss with them, as part of a plenary session, how they would tackle it. Would they need to begin the listing again? Encourage the children to predict a pattern using their knowledge of multiplication tables. All the numbers are factors of 60.

Introduce another form of transport and a time difference.

▶▶ Support

● Supply children with copies of an empty timeline, which is provided on Resource Sheet 8. Help them begin to draw a simple table or list format to record their work.

Solution

Main	8.30 a.m.
Extension	9.00 a.m.

▶ Problem

Old Macdonald plants crops of potatoes, carrots and lettuce.
The potatoes need to be harvested every 6 weeks.
The carrots need to be harvested every 28 days and the lettuces need to be harvested every 14 days.
After how many weeks will all three crops be harvested together?

NNS links	Solve mathematical problems or puzzles, recognise and explain patterns and relationships, generalise and predict. Suggest extensions by asking 'What if …?'
	Use all four operations to solve word problems involving time.

Problem-solving strategies	▪ Reason logically
	▪ Make an organised list or table

Overview	Once the strategy has been chosen the children must identify the starting point. Encourage the children to convert the times of harvest into common units of measurement, i.e. weeks rather than weeks and days. Draw the children together to establish progress being made as the problem is being solved. This will give the children the opportunity to share strategies and evaluate the strategies they are using.
	Three differentiated resource sheets are provided on the *Resources CD-ROM*. These can be used to support this activity.

▶▶ Core

Resource Sheet **a** provides the main problem for the children to solve.

Solution: All three crops can be harvested together after 12 weeks.

▶▶ Support

Resource Sheet **b** provides a table for the children to organise their information.

An alternative could be to give the children the same problem as on Resource Sheet **a** but ask the children to work on the first two elements only or use common units of measurements, weeks rather than days and weeks.

▶▶ Extension

After the children have solved the original problem, on Resource Sheet **c** they are asked to calculate the dates when the crops will be harvested and how many crops will be harvested before a certain date. A calendar would be useful for this.

Solution: a) Potatoes – 12 June, carrots – 29 May, lettuce – 15 May

b) 24 July

c) Potatoes – 4, carrots – 6, lettuce – 13

Unit 7

▶ Problem

The Number 2, Number 7 and Number 33 buses leave the bus station together at 10 a.m. Their journey times are for return journeys.
The Number 2 bus journey takes 20 minutes.
The Number 7 bus journey takes 15 minutes and the Number 33 bus journey takes 1 hour 30 minutes.
They each leave again after a 5-minute stop.
What is the next time that all three buses will be in the station together?

NNS links

Solve mathematical problems or puzzles, recognise and explain patterns and relationships, generalise and predict. Suggest extensions by asking 'What if ...?'

Use all four operations to solve word problems involving time.

Problem-solving strategies

■ Reason logically

■ Make an organised list or table

Overview

The problem will allow children practice in making an organised list and drawing a table. Once the strategy has been chosen the children must identify the starting point. Encourage the children to consider the times of the bus journeys and convert the times of the journeys into a common unit of measurement, i.e. minutes rather than mixed units, hours/minutes. Draw the children together to establish progress being made as the problem is being solved. This will give the children the opportunity to share strategies and evaluate the strategies they are using.

Three differentiated resource sheets are provided on the *Resources CD-ROM*. These can be used to support this activity.

▶▶ Core

Resource Sheet **a** presents the main problem.

Solution: The three buses will be in the bus station together at 11.35.

▶▶ Support

Resource Sheet **b** is simplified by using different timings for buses. This will result in a different solution to the problem.

Solution: 10.40

▶▶ Extension

The problem is extended by asking the children to draw up a timetable for the day for three buses and identify the times throughout the day when all three buses leave the bus station together over a 12- or 24-hour period. Children are asked to use 24-hour clock times to extend the problem further.

Solution: The table should show the following times: 12.30, 15.00, 17.30, 20.00, 22.30.

▶ **Problem**

Jacob is making lemonade for a party.
He has a 5-cup measure and a 3-cup measure.
He needs to measure out 17 cups of water.
How will he do this using only these measures?

NNS links

Solve mathematical problems or puzzles, recognise and explain patterns and relationships, generalise and predict. Suggest extensions by asking 'What if …?'

Explain methods and reasoning about numbers, orally and in writing.

Choose and use appropriate number operations and appropriate ways of calculating to solve problems.

Problem-solving strategies

- Trial and improvement
- Act out the situation

Overview

An activity that involves the children in identifying different combinations for making a target number. The measuring utensils they can use limit numbers the children can work with. The problem can be solved practically using the strategies 'act out the situation' and 'trial and improvement' or can be worked out using jottings and mental calculations. Most children will employ a combination of both. The extension activity poses a 'What if…?' question and the children will refine the methods used in the first activity to solve the second problem.

Resources

Lesson A
Interactive whiteboard
Can Do Problem-solving Year 5/P6 Whiteboard CD-ROM
Individual pupil whiteboards (or paper) and pens
Two containers – one that holds three cups of water; another that holds five cups (optional)
Plastic cup – one per group (optional)

Lesson B
General Resource Sheet A and General Resource Sheet B – enlarged or copied onto OHT
Flip chart or board
Individual pupil whiteboards (or paper) and pens
Two containers – one that holds three cups of water; another that holds five cups
Plastic cup – one per group

Follow-up problems

The Rabbit Hutch
Big Burgers

▶ Introduction

Begin by revising the problem-solving process. Click on the Five steps button to show this on the whiteboard screen.

Read and think

SCREEN 1
This screen presents the text of the problem and sets the the context of the problem.

Show The Party problem on the whiteboard. Give the children time to read the problem line by line. Ask the children to explain the problem to a partner. Prompt for understanding:

What information are you given?

What information do you need to solve the problem?

Ensure that the children are able to identify the key items of information.

Choose a strategy

Revise the nine problem-solving strategies by clicking on the Strategies button on the whiteboard screen.

Which strategies would be appropriate for this problem and which would not?

Allow a couple of minutes for children to discuss the range of suitable strategies with their partners. Appropriate strategies offered should include 'act out the situation' and 'trial and improvement'. Discuss using these strategies to solve the problem. You might also suggest at this stage that they use a combination of jottings and mental calculations. 'Acting out the situation' in this example would involve using containers of water.

Experiment

SCREEN 2
The screen contains the jug and two cups. Press Fill to fill the cups. Drag and drop the cups to the top of the jug to empty them. Cups can also be emptied into each other in the same way. The Clear button allows the jug to be emptied.

Demonstrate the method of filling, and empty the cups into the jug and into each other.

Encourage the children to record their findings using jottings. If necessary, prompt the children to consider using subtraction as well as addition to find the total of 17 using 3 and 5.

When the experimentation stage has been completed, the children should come to the whiteboard to test out their combinations of 3- and 5-cup measures to find a solution for 17 cups.

If this is being done as a practical experiment organise the children into groups and allow them to experiment with the cup and the two containers.

continued

Consider

Using children's strategies, demonstrate with the 3- and 5-cup measures how to measure 2 cups. (Fill the 3-cup measure from a 5-cup measure. Two cups will be left in the 5-cup measure.)

Does this help with your solutions?

Check on children's methods of recording and initial combinations.

Can you improve on the methods you used or the solutions that you reached?

Report and record

Look back to the problem. Ask for the children's solutions to the original problem.

Does this solution answer the question? Is this the only solution?

Ask the children to record various solutions on the whiteboard.

Demonstrate on the whiteboard that it is more effective to work out the strategy before 'acting out the situation' and that using mental calculations and jottings is an important part of trial and improvement. Give the children time to evaluate their strategies with their partners.

If you were to solve a similar problem in the future how would you adapt your strategies?

Would you use anyone else's strategy or approach in organising information?

▶▶ Extension

> **EXTENSION SCREEN**
> This screen offers the same features as Screen 2.

What if you needed to measure 22 cupfuls of lemonade?

Ask the children how they would solve the problem.

Would you use the same strategies again?

Give the children time to experiment using jottings or mental calculations, as well as by acting out the situation. Solutions can then be recorded on the whiteboard.

▶▶ Support

- Allow children to 'act out the situation' using measuring apparatus.
- Support could be given to help children explain their experimentation and record their results.

Solution

Main
  a) Four × 3-cup + one × 5-cup = 17 cups.
  b) Three × 5-cup or five × 3-cup = 15 cups.
    Then fill the 3-cup measure from a full 5-cup measure. Two cupfuls will be left in the 5-cup measure. Add these to the 15 cups already measured = 17 cups.
    Accept any other reasonable method of solving the problem.

Extension
  22 cupfuls can be measured out as follows:
  Four × 5-cup measures = 20.
  Fill the 5-cup measure and pour it into the 3-cup measure.
  Then pour the remaining 2 cups into the jug = 22.
  Again, accept any other reasonable method of solving the problem.

Unit 8 — LESSON B

▶ Introduction

Begin by revising the problem-solving process. Enlarge a copy of General Resource Sheet A to show these.

Read and think

Write The Party problem on the whiteboard. Give the children time to read the problem line by line. Ask the children to explain the problem to a partner in her/his own words. Prompt for understanding:

What information are you given?

What information do you need to solve the problem?

Ensure that the children are able to identify the key items of information.

Choose a strategy

Revise the nine problem-solving strategies by referring to General Resource Sheet B.

Which strategies would be appropriate for this problem and which would not?

Allow a couple of minutes for children to discuss the range of suitable strategies with their partners. Appropriate strategies offered should include 'act out the situation' and 'trial and improvement'. Discuss using these strategies to solve the problem. You might also suggest at this stage that they use a combination of jottings and mental calculations. 'Acting out the situation' in this example would involve using containers of water.

Experiment

Organise the children into groups and allow the children to experiment with the cup and the two containers. Encourage the children to record their findings using jottings. If necessary, prompt the children to consider using subtraction as well as addition to find the total of 17 using 3 and 5.

When the experimentation stage has been completed, the children could come to the board or flip chart to test their combinations of 3- and 5-cup measures to find a solution for 17 cups.

Consider

Using children's strategies, demonstrate with the 3- and 5-cup measures how to measure 2 cups. (Fill the 3-cup measure from a 5-cup measure. Two cups will be left in the 5-cup measure.)

Does this help with your solutions?

Check on children's methods of recording and initial combinations.

Can you improve on the methods you used or the solutions that you reached?

continued

Report and record

Look back to the problem. Ask for the children's solutions to the original problem.

Does this solution answer the question? Is this the only solution?

Ask the children to record various solutions on the board or flip chart.

Establish through a demonstration on the board or flip chart that it is more effective to work out the strategy before 'acting out the situation' and that using mental calculations and jottings is an important part of trial and improvement.

Give the children time to reflect and evaluate their strategies with their partners.

If you were to solve a similar problem in the future how would you adapt your strategies?

Would you use anyone else's strategy or approach in organising information?

▶▶ Extension

What if you needed to measure 22 cupfuls of lemonade?

Ask the children how they would solve the problem.

Would you use the same strategies again?

Give the children time to experiment using jottings or mental calculations, as well as by acting out the situation. Solutions can then be recorded on the whiteboard. They can illustrate their solutions practically if necessary.

▶▶ Support

● Allow children to 'act out the situation' using measuring apparatus.

● Support could be given to help children explain their experimentation and record their results.

Solution

Main
Four × 3-cup + one × 5-cup = 17 cups.
Three × 5-cup or five × 3-cup = 15 cups.
Then fill the 3-cup measure from a full 5-cup measure. Two cupfuls will be left in the 5-cup measure. Add these to the 15 cups already measured = 17 cups.
Accept any other reasonable method of solving the problem.

Extension
22 cupfuls can be measured out as follows:
Four × 5-cup measures = 20.
Fill the 5-cup measure and pour it into the 3-cup measure.
Then pour the remaining 2 cups into the jug = 22.
Again, accept any other reasonable method of solving the problem.

▶ *Problem*

Alex and Lucy are building a rabbit hutch with their father.

The rabbit hutch needs to measure 1·3 m wide in order to be large enough for the rabbit.

Dad's measuring tape measures in 20 cm intervals on one side and 50 cm intervals on the other.

How can they ensure the hutch is the correct size?

NNS links	Solve mathematical problems or puzzles, recognise and explain patterns and relationships, generalise and predict. Suggest extensions by asking 'What if …?'
	Explain methods and reasoning about numbers, orally and in writing.
	Choose and use appropriate number operations and appropriate ways of calculating to solve problems.

Problem-solving strategies	▓ Trial and improvement
	▓ Draw a picture or diagram or make a model

Overview	A problem-solving activity that involves the children in identifying different combinations for making a target number. The context is making a rabbit hutch and the measuring tape limits numbers the children can work with. Children should be encouraged to convert 1·3 m into centimetres before they begin. Suitable strategies could include 'draw a diagram' and 'trial and improvement'. They should also use jottings and mental calculations to explore different combinations of measurements. Most children will employ a combination of both. The extension activity asks them to do the same for the height of the hutch and also to identify measurements that cannot be made.
	Three differentiated resource sheets are provided on the *Resources CD-ROM*. These can be used to support this activity.

continued

▶▶ *Core*

Resource Sheet **a** presents the main problem.

Solution:
50 cm + 50 cm + 50 cm − 20 cm = 130 cm. Accept any other reasonable answer to the problem.

▶▶ *Support*

Emphasise the use of number bonds to create totals. Allow children to make their own measuring tapes to explore the problem.

Resource Sheet **b** gives the measurements of the rabbit hutch in centimetres.

▶▶ *Extension*

Resource Sheet **c** presents two additional problems.

Solution:

None, they can all be measured.

10 cm = 50 cm − 20 cm − 20 cm

20 cm = 20 cm

30 cm = 50 cm − 20 cm

40 cm = 2 × 20 cm

50 cm = 50 cm

60 cm = 3 × 20 cm

70 cm = 50 cm + 20 cm

80 cm = 4 × 20 cm

90 cm = 50 cm + 20 cm + 20 cm

1 m = 50 cm + 50 cm

▶ Problem

The Burger Bar is very busy.

Hassan has already sold 55 meals since he started work.

Some people ordered meals containing single burgers, some with double burgers and some with triple burgers.

He sold 4 more singles than doubles.

If he has sold a total of 103 burgers, how many meals contained single burgers, how many contained double burgers and how many contained triple burgers?

NNS links

Solve mathematical problems or puzzles, recognise and explain patterns and relationships, generalise and predict. Suggest extensions by asking 'What if …?'

Explain methods and reasoning about numbers, orally and in writing.

Choose and use appropriate number operations and appropriate ways of calculating to solve problems.

Problem-solving strategies

■ Trial and improvement

■ Reason logically

Overview

An activity that involves the children in identifying different combinations for making a target number. The context is a Burger Bar. The most appropriate strategy is 'trial and improvement'. Children should use this strategy in a systematic way, refining initial attempts to inform further calculations. These can be worked out using jottings and mental calculations. Most children will employ a combination of both.

Three differentiated resource sheets are provided on the *Resources CD-ROM*. These can be used to support this activity.

▶▶ Core

Resource Sheet **a** presents the main problem.

Solution: 22 singles, 18 doubles, 15 triples ($22 + (18 \times 2) + (15 \times 3) = 103$ burgers).

▶▶ Support

A simplified version of the main problem is presented on Resource Sheet **b**.

Solution: 5 single and 20 double.

▶▶ Extension

An additional problem using the same context is given on Resource Sheet **c**. Children have all the information they need to solve this and need to choose the appropriate number operations to solve it.

Solution: £43·89.

Unit 9 TOWER HEIGHTS

▶ **Problem**

The Jones family were planning a trip to Tower Heights. The last part of the journey took them through several small villages. Mrs Jones wanted to find the shortest route. From Cheadle how should she go to Tower Heights?

Route A via Oakmoor and Bradley

or

Route B via Denstone, Farley and Edgehill?

NNS links

Use all four operations to solve word problems involving length.

Choose and use appropriate number operations and appropriate ways of calculating to solve problems.

Explain methods and reasoning about numbers, orally and in writing.

Problem-solving strategies

▪ Make a conjecture and test it with particular examples

▪ Draw a picture or diagram or make a model

Overview

This problem encourages the children to make a conjecture, or hypothesis, about a problem and then test their conjecture using examples. It will involve children reviewing their conjectures according to their results, and also attempting to test their conjecture more than once to ensure the results are the same and accurate.

The children should be able to work with adding lengths involving one decimal place. They will also estimate distances, rounding to the nearest whole number before they do so.

Resources

Lesson A
Interactive whiteboard
Can Do Problem-solving Year 5/P6 Whiteboard CD-ROM
Resource Sheet 9 Map 1
Individual pupil whiteboards (or paper) and pens

Lesson B
General Resource Sheet A and General Resource Sheet B – enlarged or copied onto OHT
Resource Sheet 9 Map 1
Resource Sheet 10 Map 2
Individual pupil whiteboards and pens

Follow-up problems

Tower Heights Prices
The Rides

▶ *Introduction*

Begin by revising the problem-solving process. Click on the Five steps button to show this screen.

Read and think

Show the Tower Heights problem on the whiteboard. Give the children time to read the problem. Ask the children to explain the problem to their partners in their own words. Prompt for understanding:

What information are you given?

What information do you need to solve the problem?

Ensure that the children are able to identify the key items of information.

SCREEN 1
Allow time for the children to read the text before proceeding. The problem is animated with a car driving along the two routes on the map suggested in Route A and Route B. Press Play for the animation to proceed.

Choose a strategy

Revise the nine problem-solving strategies by clicking on the Strategies button on the screen.

Which strategies would be appropriate for this problem and which would not?

Allow a couple of minutes for children to discuss the range of suitable strategies with their partners.

Appropriate strategies offered should include 'make a conjecture and test it with particular examples' and 'draw a picture or diagram or make a model'.

Discuss with the class the strategy of making a conjecture (or hypothesis). Relate it to work in other subject areas – for example, science, where conjectures are made and tests are set up to prove or disprove the conjecture. State that it does not matter whether our conjecture is right or wrong so long as it is a reasonable conjecture.

Ask the children to make a conjecture about the Tower Heights problem.

Which plan appears to be the shortest way to complete the journey?

Children can be asked to estimate the distances to help form their conjecture. Distances can be estimated using the rounded distances if desired.

SCREEN 1
Click in the box to make a conjecture about the shortest route. Click on the Round button to show distances rounded to the nearest kilometre.

Ask each child to write 'Route A' or 'Route B' on their whiteboards and show their decision to the rest of the class. Use the majority decision and check in the box for Route A or Route B.

continued

Experiment

Using Screen 2, allow the children to come to the whiteboard and demonstrate the movement of the car as it 'drives' along the route. Distances can again be rounded and answers estimated if desired. Allow children time to work out which route is shortest.

Allow the children to record the distances for both routes and which route was shortest, using either actual or rounded distances.

SCREEN 2
The map on this screen can be used to plot Route A and Route B. Click on the 'road' to highlight the section between villages. Use the keypad to enter distances in the boxes for Route A and Route B.

Consider

Ask the children to consider whether they would have obtained the same result if the answers had been worked out using rounded and actual distances.

Report and record

Bring the class together and show the Solution screen. Compare the result with the conjectures given at the beginning of the session.

SOLUTION SCREEN
Press Play to run the animation, which shows the distances being calculated and entered in the totals box.

▶▶ *Extension*

EXTENSION SCREEN
A new map and the extension problem are shown.

A new map is shown with an additional village. Children are asked to find two new routes to Tower Heights and then make a conjecture about whether Route B is still the shortest. Children can identify the two new routes on the whiteboard and describe them. (There are also others but these can be discussed and discarded since they are obviously longer.) Ask children to make a conjecture about which route is now shortest. Allow the children time to experiment and

work out the solution. Ask them to write on their individual whiteboards the total distances for both routes and which route was shortest. Rounded or actual measurements can be used. Ask individuals to enter their calculations in the totals box.

Finally, compare the result of the two new calculations with the conjectures given at the beginning of the extension activity.

▶▶ *Support*

● Allow children to calculate the distance using whole numbers. These can be written on Resource Sheet 9 Map 1. Distances rounded to the nearest kilometre can be shown on Screen 2.

Solution

See also the Solution screen.

Main   Route A is 20·8 km.
Route B is 19·5 km so Route B is shorter.
The same solution would apply if rounded measurements were used.

Extension   The route via Ernstone is 16·7 km.
The route via Ernstone, Farley and Edgehill is also 16·7 km.
Therefore both these routes are shorter than the original conjecture.

Unit 9 LESSON B

▶ **Introduction**

Begin by revising the problem-solving process. Show an enlarged version of General Resource Sheet A to do this.

Read and think

Write the Tower Heights problem on the whiteboard and give out copies of Resource Sheet 9 – Map 1. Give the children time to read the problem line by line. Ask the class to explain the problem to a partner in her/his own words. Prompt for understanding:

What information are you given?

What information do you need to solve the problem?

Ensure that the children are able to identify the key items of information.

Choose a strategy

Revise the nine problem-solving strategies by enlarging General Resource Sheet B or copying it onto OHT.

Which strategies would be appropriate for this problem and which would not?

Allow a couple of minutes for children to discuss the range of suitable strategies with their partner.

Appropriate strategies offered should include 'make a conjecture and test it with particular examples' and 'draw a picture or diagram or make a model'.

Discuss with the class the strategy of making a conjecture (or hypothesis). Relate to work in other subject areas – for example, science, where conjectures are made and tests are set up to prove or disprove the conjecture. State that it does not matter whether our conjecture is right or wrong so long as it is a reasonable conjecture.

Ask the children to make a conjecture about the Tower Heights problem.

Which plan appears to be the shortest way to complete the journey?

Discuss with the class what they have to find out. Children should tell you that it is the shortest route to Tower Heights that they will need to find out.

Children can be asked to estimate the distances to help form their conjecture. To do this they might want to round the measurements to the nearest kilometre.

Ask each child to write 'Plan A' or 'Plan B' on their individual whiteboards and show their decision to the rest of the class.

continued

Experiment

Allow the children time to experiment and work out which route is shortest. Ask children to write on their individual whiteboards the distances for both routes and which route was shortest.

Compare the result with the conjectures given at the beginning of the session.

Consider

Ask the children to consider whether they would have obtained the same result if the answers had been worked out using rounded and estimated distances.

Report and record

Ask individual children to record their working in writing on the board or flip chart.

▶▶ Extension

A new map is shown on Resource Sheet 10 Map 2 with an additional village. Children are asked to find two new routes to Tower Heights and then make a conjecture about whether Route B is still the shortest. Children can identify the two new routes. There are also others but these can be discussed and discarded since they are obviously longer. Ask children to make a conjecture about which route is now shortest. Allow children time to experiment and work out the solution. Ask children to write on their individual whiteboards the total distances for both routes and which route was shortest.

Rounded or actual measurements can be used.

Compare the result of the two new calculations with the conjectures given at the beginning of the session.

▶▶ Support

● Allow children to calculate the distance using whole numbers. These can be written on Resource Sheet 9 Map 1. Distances rounded to the nearest kilometre can be shown on Screen 2.

Solution

Main   Route A is 20·8 km.
         Route B is 19·5 km so Route B is shorter.
         The same solution would apply if rounded measurements were used.

Extension   The route via Ernstone is 16·7 km.
           The route via Ernstone, Farley and Edgehill is also 16·7 km.
           Therefore both these routes are shorter than the original conjecture.

▶ **Problem**

There are five people in the Jones family: Mum and Dad, Tom 12, Alice 10 and Sophie 4. There are two ways to pay to get into Tower Heights.

Family Ticket
Up to 5 people £37·50
Children must be under 16

Prices
Adult: £10·50
Children 5–16 £6·50
Children 0–4 free

To get in the cheapest way, should the Jones family buy the family ticket or not?

NNS links

Use all four operations to solve word problems involving money.

Choose and use appropriate number operations and appropriate ways of calculating to solve problems.

Explain methods and reasoning about numbers, orally and in writing.

Problem-solving strategies

▨ Make a conjecture and test it with particular examples

Overview

This problem continues the theme park context and presents two different conjectures for the children to test out given the number of people in the Jones family. They will be using calculations involving money and may need to use pencil and paper methods to solve the problem. Three differentiated resource sheets are provided on the *Resources CD-ROM*. These can be used to support this activity.

▶▶ **Core**

Resource Sheet **a** presents the main problem.

Solution:
No they should not buy the family ticket.

▶▶ **Support**

On Resource Sheet **b** children are asked to work out the cost of entry on individual prices only. The family ticket and comparison can be introduced afterwards if desired. Alternatively children can be given additional adult help to complete the core problem.

Solution: It costs £34·00 for the Jones family to get in.

▶▶ **Extension**

On Resource Sheet **c** children solve the main problem and then a 'What if …?' question is added where another family group is introduced and the children are required to test whether this group should buy the family ticket or not.

Solution: Yes they should buy the family ticket.

Unit 9   FOLLOW-UP PROBLEM: THE RIDES

► **Problem**

> The Big One – 45 mins
> The Gravity Pull – 55 mins
> Log Flume – 32 mins
> Corkscrew – 1 hr 05 mins
> Black Hole – 20 mins
> Enterprise – 1 hr
> Runaway Train – 10 mins
> X-Ride – 38 mins

The rides at Tower Heights are very busy. Tom and Alice want to spend as little time queuing as possible.
Should they choose to go on:
a) The Big One, the Log Flume, the Corkscrew, the Runaway Train and the Black Hole
or
b) The Gravity Pull, the Enterprise, the X-Ride, the Log Flume and the Black Hole?

NNS links

Use all four operations to solve word problems involving time.

Choose and use appropriate number operations and appropriate ways of calculating to solve problems.

Explain methods and reasoning about numbers, orally and in writing.

Problem-solving strategies

■ Make a conjecture and test it with particular examples

Overview

This problem continues the theme park context and presents two different conjectures for the children to test out given that Tom and Alice want to spend as little time queuing as possible. They will be using calculations involving time and may need to use pencil and paper methods to solve the problem.

Three differentiated resource sheets are provided on the *Resources CD-ROM*. These can be used to support this activity.

continued

Core

Resource Sheet **a** presents the problem.

Solution: a) would mean they would spend
172 minutes queuing.
b) would mean 205 minutes
queuing.
Therefore they should choose a).

Support

Children are presented with a simpler list of
times to work with on Resource Sheet **b**.
They could also work on the core problem
with adult help.

Solution: a) would mean they had to queue
for 115 minutes.
b) would mean they had to queue
for 100 minutes.
Therefore they should choose b).

Extension

Children work on the main problem and then
a 'What if …?' problem is presented on
Resource Sheet **c**. The queuing times of
some of the rides are increased and
decreased. Children have to re-examine their
conjectures and test them against the
original.

Solution: They should still choose a).
Option a) is 177 minutes and
b) is 210 minutes.

Each of the two lists contains one
ride where the queueing time has
increased and one where it has
decreased, so the effect on the
total time is the same for both lists.

Five Steps to Problem-solving

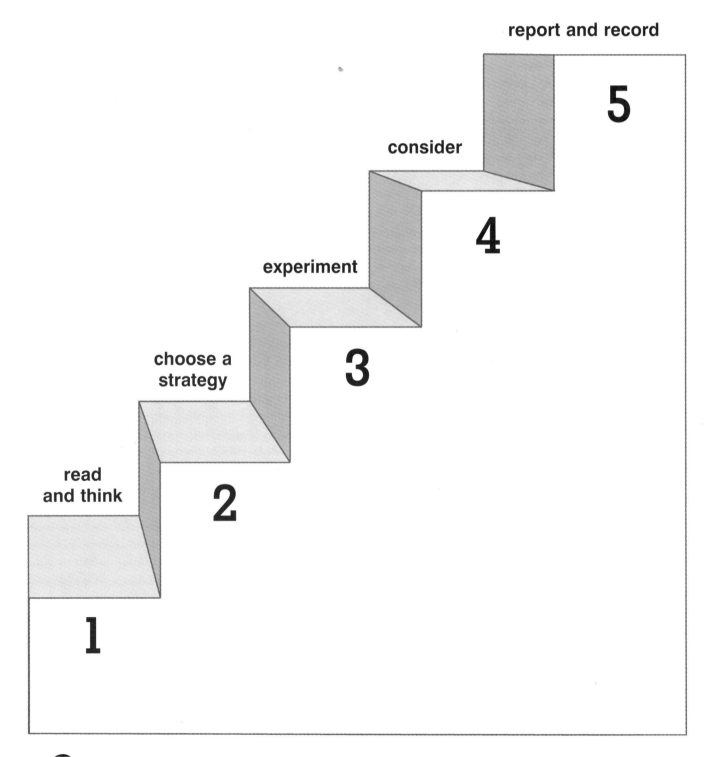

report and record

5

consider

4

experiment

3

choose a
strategy

2

read
and think

1

Problem-solving Strategies

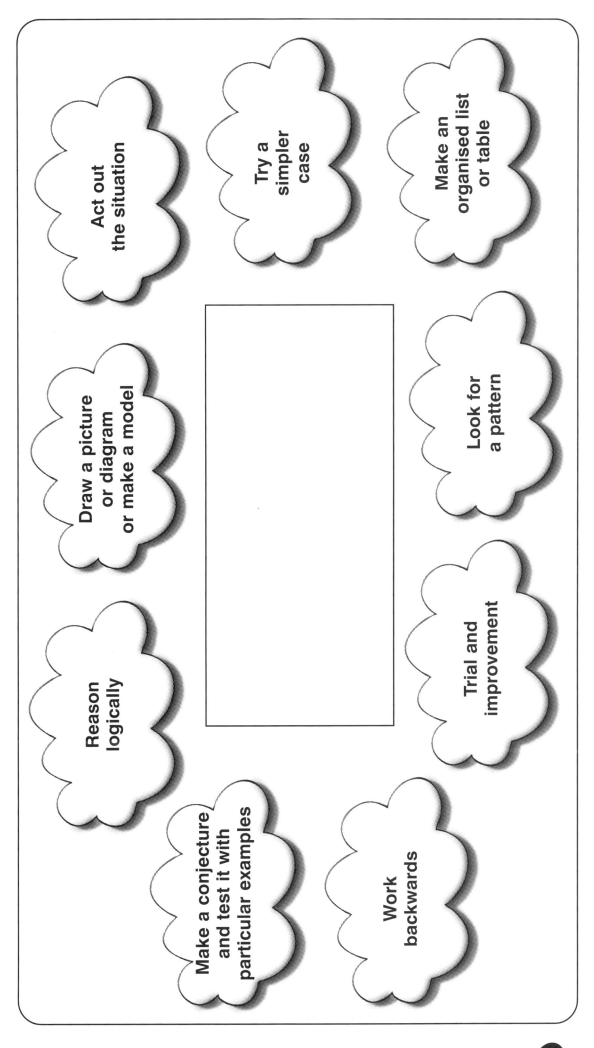

Act out
the situation

Try a
simpler
case

Make an
organised list
or table

Draw a picture
or diagram
or make a model

Look for
a pattern

Reason
logically

Trial and
improvement

Make a conjecture
and test it with
particular examples

Work
backwards

Table Plan and Clues

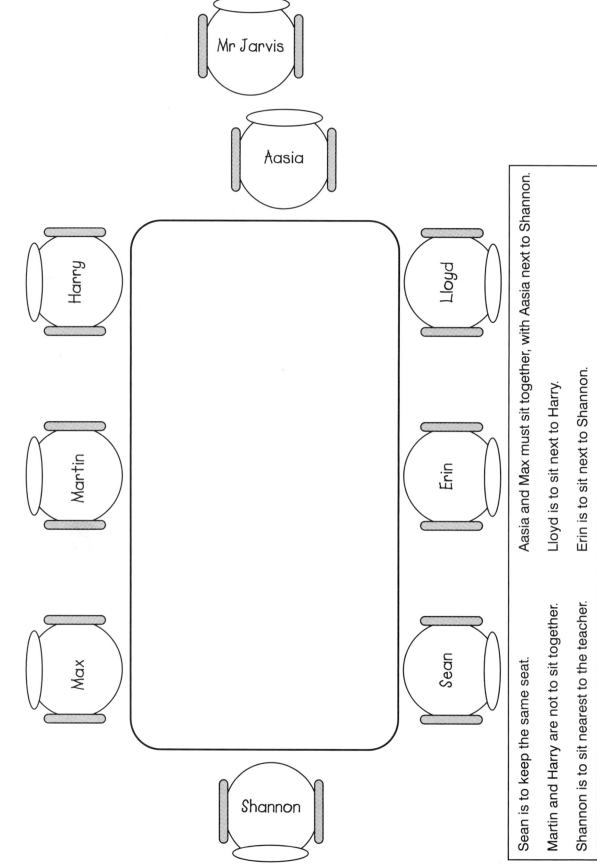

Mr Jarvis

Aasia

Harry

Lloyd

Martin

Erin

Max

Sean

Shannon

Sean is to keep the same seat.

Martin and Harry are not to sit together.

Shannon is to sit nearest to the teacher.

Aasia and Max must sit together, with Aasia next to Shannon.

Lloyd is to sit next to Harry.

Erin is to sit next to Shannon.

Table Plan and Names

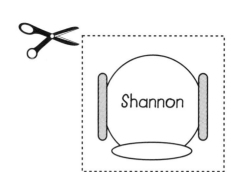
Shannon

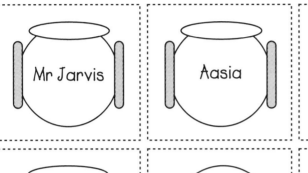
Mr Jarvis | Aasia

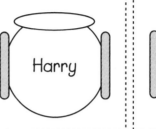
Harry

Lloyd

Martin | Erin | Max | Sean

Table

The Football League

Number of teams	Number of games

Aliens

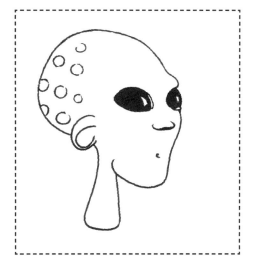

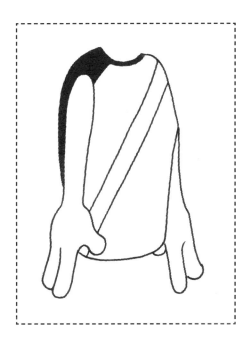

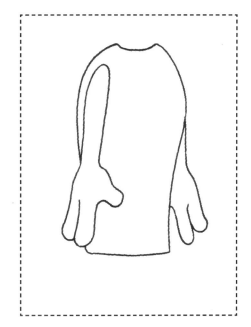

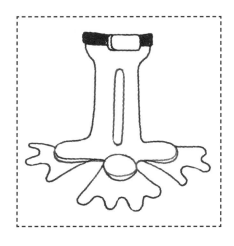

Craig's Telephone Number

CAN DO PROBLEM-SOLVING Year 5/P6 © Sarah Foster and Lynsey Ankers, Nelson Thornes Ltd, 2004

Peter's Telephone Number

Now it's Craig's turn to work out Peter's number

Use the clues to work out Peter's number

Clue 1: There are four digits.

Clue 2: The second number is three times bigger than the first.

Clue 3: If you subtract the third digit from the second, you get the fourth.

Clue 4: The total of the first and fourth digits is eight.

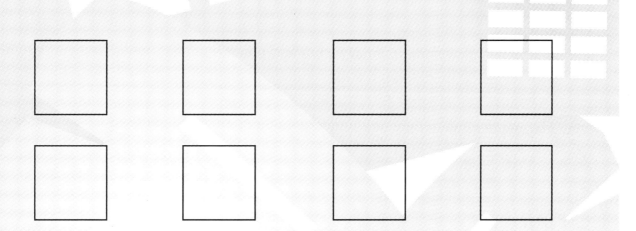

The Rucksack

Candlestick 4 kg £30

Crown 2 kg £50

Gold bar 8 kg £120

Bag of silver coins 3 kg £20

Statue 6 kg £90

Timeline

6 minutes

8.00	8.05	8.10	8.15	8.20	8.25	8.30	8.35	8.40	8.45

10 minutes

8.00	8.05	8.10	8.15	8.20	8.25	8.30	8.35	8.40	8.45

15 minutes

8.00	8.05	8.10	8.15	8.20	8.25	8.30	8.35	8.40	8.45

Map 1

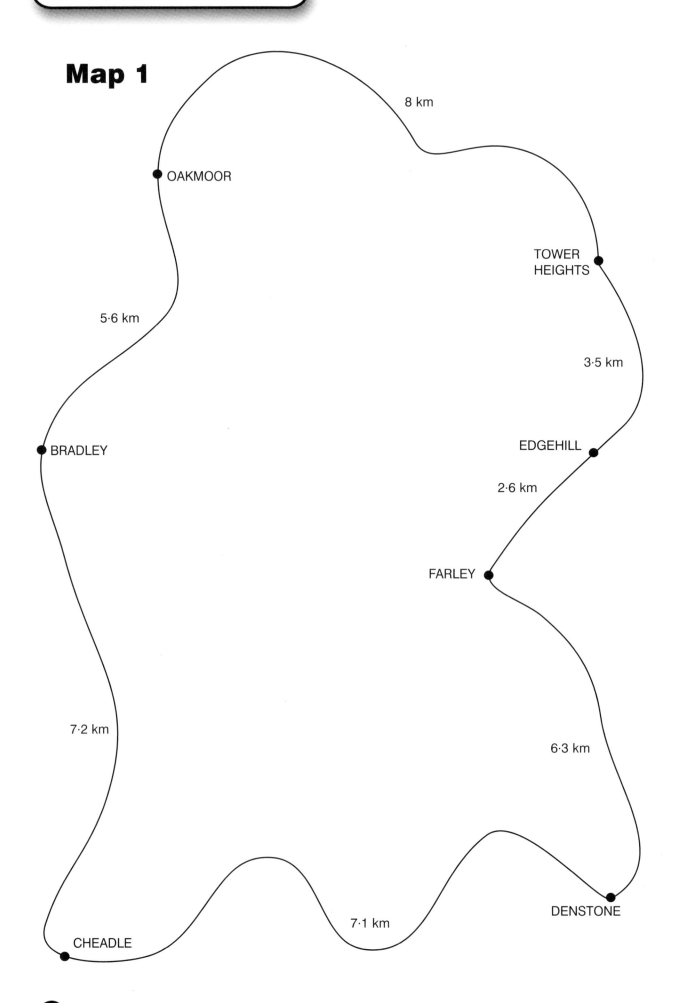

8 km

OAKMOOR

TOWER
HEIGHTS

5·6 km

3·5 km

BRADLEY

EDGEHILL

2·6 km

FARLEY

7·2 km

6·3 km

DENSTONE

7·1 km

CHEADLE

Map 2

The map now shows the village of Ernstone. Can you find two new routes to get to Tower Heights? Is Route B still the shortest route to Tower Heights?

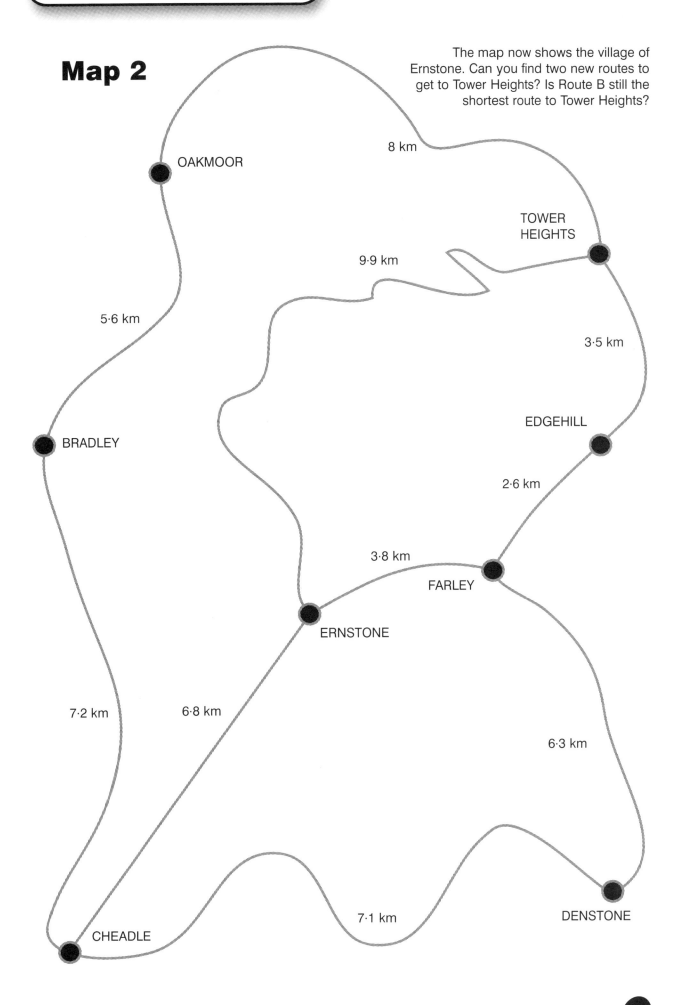

OAKMOOR

8 km

TOWER HEIGHTS

9·9 km

5·6 km

3·5 km

EDGEHILL

BRADLEY

2·6 km

3·8 km

FARLEY

ERNSTONE

7·2 km

6·8 km

6·3 km

7·1 km

DENSTONE

CHEADLE

Can Do

Problem-solving

SECTION 2

Problems Bank

Problems Bank Correlation Chart

Problem	Choose and use appropriate number operations…	Explain methods and reasoning…	Make and investigate a general statement…	Express a relationship…	Solve mathematical problems or puzzles…	Use all four operations … 'real life'	Use all four operations … money	Use all four operations …length, mass or capacity	Use all four operations … time	Reason about shape	c = calculator	Mathematical content
1 The Farm					●							logic
2 Shopping					●							logic
3 Tower of Bricks					●							logic
4 Roundabout					●							number deduction puzzle
5 Deliveries					●							number deduction puzzle
6 At the Supermarket					●	●						number deduction puzzle
7 Chess					●							number deduction puzzle
8 Table Tennis					●							number deduction puzzle
9 The Ghost Train					●							listing all possibilities
10 Code Cracker	●				●							number deduction puzzle
11 Consecutive Numbers (1)					●							consecutive number puzzle
12 Consecutive Numbers (2)					●							consecutive number puzzle
13 The Sweet Shop	●	●					●					comparison of calculations
14 Boats					●							logic
15 Odd Shoes					●							logic
16 Window View								●				calculations involving length
17 Frame It								●		●		calculations involving length and perimeter
18 Squares and Rectangles		●								●		calculations involving length and perimeter
19 Pathway Patterns		●								●		length and patterns
20 Cycle Hire							●					calculations involving money and quantities
21 Water Bottles							●				c	calculations involving money and quantities
22 Jigsaw Fun		●				●						calculations involving money and quantities
23 Letter Values					●							addition, odd and even numbers
24 Visit to the Theme Park		●				●						calculating quantities
25 Count the Spots					●							calculating and deducing quantities
26 Logical Thinking					●							logic, deducing numbers
27 In My Head	●		●									number deduction puzzles
28 Pick a Number (1)	●				●							number puzzles
29 Pick a Number (2)	●				●							number puzzles
30 Even It Up (1)					●							equal total puzzle
31 Even It Up (2)					●							equal total puzzle
32 Even It Up (3)					●							equal total puzzle
33 Cross Country									●		c	calculations involving time
34 Time Conversions		●							●		c	calculations involving time
35 Number Rules			●									number sequences
36 Bus Stop									●			calculations involving time
37 A Question of Length		●						●			c	calculations involving length
38 From the Ice Box							●					calculations involving money
39 Savings							●				c	calculations involving money

Problem	Choose and use appropriate number operations …	Explain methods and reasoning …	Make and investigate a general statement …	Express a relationship …	Solve mathematical problems or puzzles …	Use all four operations … 'real life'	Use all four operations … money	Use all four operations … length, mass or capacity	Use all four operations … time	Reason about shape	c = calculator	Mathematical content
					NNS links							
40 Missing Numbers		●									c	missing number calculations
41 True, False or Sometimes True? (1)		●	●								c	reasoning about number statements
42 Back to the Beginning					●							number deduction puzzles
43 A Question of Position										●		perimeter problems
44 Squares within Squares		●			●						c	number patterns, addition
45 Consecutive Numbers (3)		●	●									consecutive number puzzles
46 At the Youth Club						●	●					calculations involving money and quantities
47 Party Time							●	●				calculations involving money and capacity
48 Hot Dog Van							●				c	calculations involving money
49 Egg Boxes						●					c	calculations involving quantities
50 A Good Read		●				●						calculations involving quantities
51 School Concert	●					●					c	calculations involving money and quantities
52 On the Slate										●		calculations involving 2D dimensions
53 Fill Me								●				calculations involving capacity
54 Weighing Scales								●				calculations involving weight
55 April 2004									●			using and interpreting a calendar
56 Monday's Timetable									●			using and interpreting a timetable
57 Car Boot Sale							●					calculations involving money
58 The Sandwich Shop							●					calculations involving money
59 Sponsored Run							●					calculations involving money
60 Phone Bills							●		●			calculations involving time and money
61 At the Round Pound Shop							●					calculations involving money
62 True, False or Sometimes True? (2)		●	●								c	reasoning about numbers and shapes
63 Number Pairs				●							c	total, product, difference and sum
64 Sensible or Silly?								●				reasoning about measurements of length
65 Can You Make Me?				●								testing calculations
66 Mr Rimmer's New Lawn						●					c	calculating quantities
67 Sticker Fun						●					c	calculating quantities
68 Leftovers								●			c	calculating remainders
69 Newspaper Sales						●					c	interpreting data
70 Matching Up						●						deducing quantities
71 Temperature Check						●						calculations involving temperature
72 Lemonade Break								●			c	calculations involving capacity
73 Round Up or Down?						●					c	calculating quantities
74 Chicken and Mushroom Soup								●			c	adjusting quantities
75 Spot the Error						●						identifying correct and incorrect answers
76 Divisibility Tests			●									divisibility by 0, 3, 4, 5

1 The Farm

Problem

At Greenheys farm there are sheep, cows, pigs, ducks and goats in 5 different fields.

The goats are next to the house.

The pigs are next to the cows but not next to the sheep.

The cows are not beside the ducks.

The ducks are furthest away from the house.

Arrange the fields in the correct order.

NNS links

■ Solve mathematical problems or puzzles, recognise and explain patterns and relationships, generalise and predict. Suggest extensions by asking 'What if ...?'

Solution

House	or	House
Goats		Goats
Sheep		Pigs
Cows		Cows
Pigs		Sheep
Ducks		Ducks

2 Shopping

Problem

Ashley is packing the shopping into boxes.

He cannot put soap in a box with food.

He cannot put eggs in a box with tins.

Three items go in each box.

Pack the boxes.

Shopping: Fish, Soap, Tissues, Apples, Tinned peas, Soap powder, Tinned beans, Eggs, Can of orange.

NNS links

■ Solve mathematical problems or puzzles, recognise and explain patterns and relationships, generalise and predict. Suggest extensions by asking 'What if ...?'

Solution

Fish, apples, eggs

Soap, tissues, soap powder

Tinned peas, tinned beans, can of orange

3 Tower of Bricks

Problem

Benny is building a tower of five bricks.

He put the red brick on top of the green one.

He put the blue brick under the yellow one.

He put the black one in the middle under the green brick.

Which brick is on the bottom?

NNS links

■ Solve mathematical problems or puzzles, recognise and explain patterns and relationships, generalise and predict. Suggest extensions by asking 'What if ...?'

Solution

Blue

④ Roundabout

Problem

Some children were on the roundabout.

When it stopped, five of them jumped off and four more climbed on.

A further two children joined the roundabout, three children left to play on the slide and four children left to join a game of football.

There were now eleven children on the roundabout.

How many children were on the roundabout to start with?

NNS links

- Solve mathematical problems or puzzles, recognise and explain patterns and relationships, generalise and predict. Suggest extensions by asking 'What if ...?'

Solution

17

⑤ Deliveries

Problem

Tom has some parcels to deliver.

He delivers 4 parcels before lunch but is unable to deliver 6 parcels before lunch as the customers are not in.

After lunch he delivers a further 9 parcels but is unable to deliver 5 more parcels.

At the end of the day Tom is left with 25 parcels.

How many parcels did he start the day with?

NNS links

- Solve mathematical problems or puzzles, recognise and explain patterns and relationships, generalise and predict. Suggest extensions by asking 'What if ...?'

Solution

38

⑥ At the Supermarket

Problem

Gail buys a tin of beans costing 37p, a bag of apples costing £1·10, a loaf of bread for 75p, and a bar of chocolate costing 42p.

After paying for her shopping she has a five pound note, £2 and 36p in change.

How much money did she have to start with?

NNS links

- Use all four operations to solve word problems involving money.
- Solve mathematical problems or puzzles, recognise and explain patterns and relationships, generalise and predict. Suggest extensions by asking 'What if ...?'

Solution

£10

(7) Chess

Problem

There are 6 children in the school chess championships. Each child must play each of the others only once.

How many games of chess will be played?

NNS links

■ Solve mathematical problems or puzzles, recognise and explain patterns and relationships, generalise and predict. Suggest extensions by asking 'What if ...?'

Solution

15 games

---

(8) Table Tennis

Problem

There are 8 teams in the table tennis league.

Each team will play each of the others once only.

How many games will be played altogether?

NNS links

■ Solve mathematical problems or puzzles, recognise and explain patterns and relationships, generalise and predict. Suggest extensions by asking 'What if ...?'

Solution

28

---

(9) The Ghost Train

Problem

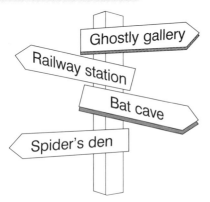

Mr Stuart is planning a route for the ghost train.

It must start at the station, visit the spider's den twice, visit all the other places once and return to the station.

List all the routes the ghost train can take.

NNS links

■ Solve mathematical problems or puzzles, recognise and explain patterns and relationships, generalise and predict. Suggest extensions by asking 'What if ...?'

Solution

S, D, C, D, G, S

S, D, G, D, C, S

S, D, C, G, D, S

S, D, G, C, D, S

S, G, D, C, D, S

S, C, D, G, D, S

(10) Code Cracker

Problem

Michael's friend has given him a code to crack. There are 5 numbers in the code.

The middle number is a square number that is also odd.

The first number is the same as the last number.

The second and fourth digits are both found in the 3 times table and add up to the middle digit.

All numbers added together total 28.

What is the code?

NNS links

■ Choose and use appropriate number operations and appropriate ways of calculating to solve problems.
■ Solve mathematical problems or puzzles, recognise and explain patterns and relationships, generalise and predict. Suggest extensions by asking 'What if ...?'

Solution

5 3 9 6 5 or 5 6 9 3 5

---

(11) Consecutive Numbers (1)

Problem

Five consecutive numbers added together total 70. What are the five numbers?

NNS links

■ Solve mathematical problems or puzzles, recognise and explain patterns and relationships, generalise and predict. Suggest extensions by asking 'What if ...?'

Solution

12, 13, 14, 15, 16

---

(12) Consecutive Numbers (2)

Problem

Three consecutive numbers total 135. What are the three numbers?

NNS links

■ Solve mathematical problems or puzzles, recognise and explain patterns and relationships, generalise and predict. Suggest extensions by asking 'What if...?'

Solution

44, 45, 46

13 The Sweet Shop

Problem

The sweet shop has special offers on the sweets.

Choco bars are 3 for the price of 2. They cost 15p each.

Chew Chew chocs cost 20p. For every bar you buy you get another half price.

Truly Scrumptious chocs have 10% off and if you buy one you get one free. They normally cost 30p each.

Which is the best offer and why?

NNS links

- Explain methods and reasoning about numbers, orally and in writing.
- Choose and use appropriate number operations and appropriate ways of calculating to solve problems.
- Use all four operations to solve word problems involving money.

Solution

Choco bars – 3 for 30p

---

14 Boats

Problem

At the lake, rowing boats can be hired for 20 minutes, pedal boats can be hired for 30 minutes and power boats can be hired for 45 minutes.

There are no gaps between hirings.

If the boat shed opens at 9 a.m. at what time will all the boats be back in the shed together?

NNS links

- Solve mathematical problems or puzzles, recognise and explain patterns and relationships, generalise and predict. Suggest extensions by asking 'What if …?'

Solution

12.00

---

15 Odd Shoes

Problem

Holly has 6 different pairs of shoes in her cupboard.

What is the least number of shoes she will have to take out of the cupboard to ensure she has a matching pair?

NNS links

- Solve mathematical problems or puzzles, recognise and explain patterns and relationships, generalise and predict. Suggest extensions by asking 'What if …?'

Solution

7 shoes

⑯ Window View

Problem

a) The blind on the window has been pulled up 1·7 metres. How much of the window does the blind still cover?

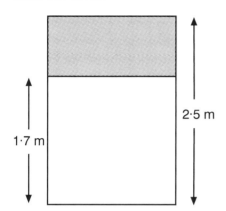

b) Each of the curtains on this window is 80 cm wide. How wide is the gap between them?

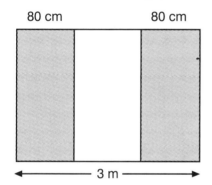

c) On the same window, the curtains are pulled back so the gap now measures 2·1 metres. If both curtains are the same width, how many centimetres wide is each?

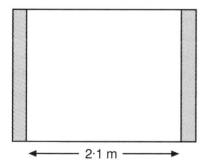

NNS links

▪ Use all four operations to solve word problems involving length, mass or capacity.

Solution

a) 80 cm

b) 140 cm or 1·4 m

c) 45 cm

17 Frame It

Problem

A rectangular picture frame is twice as long as it is wide.

a) If the frame is 16 cm wide, what is its length?

b) If the frame is 14 cm long, what is its perimeter?

c) If the perimeter is 30 cm, what is its length?

A second frame is three times as long as it is wide.

d) If the frame is 8 cm wide, what is its length?

e) If the frame is 36 cm long, what is its perimeter?

f) If the perimeter is 80 cm, what is its width?

NNS links

■ Use all four operations to solve word problems involving length, mass or capacity.

■ Reason about shape.

Solution

a) 32 cm

b) 42 cm

c) 10 cm

d) 24 cm

e) 96 cm

f) 10 cm

---

18 Squares and Rectangles

Problem

Ravi had a collection of squares and rectangles and used these to make the shape below.

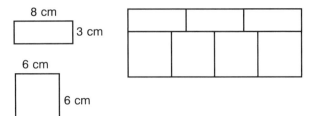

a) What is the length (l) of the new shape?

b) What is the breadth (b) of the shape?

c) Calculate the perimeter of the shape.

Ravi says, 'If I continue the pattern and add 6 more squares and 5 more rectangles to the length, the new shape will be a rectangle which is 60 cm long.' Is he correct? Explain your answer.

NNS links

■ Explain methods and reasoning about numbers, orally and in writing.

■ Reason about shape.

Solution

a) 24 cm

b) 9 cm

c) 66 cm

d) No – 6 more squares will give a length of 60 cm, but 5 more rectangles will give a length of 64 cm. The new shape will not be a rectangle.

Mr Anderson was building a path using rectangular slabs as shown:

80 cm

40 cm

He began the path like this:

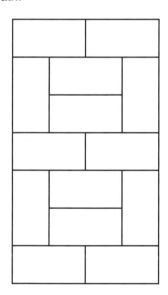

a) What is the length of this section?

Mr Anderson added 6 more slabs to extend the path:

b) What is the new length of the path?

c) Continuing the same pattern, what is the total number of slabs Mr Anderson will need to extend the length of his path to 4 metres?

d) 'If I continue adding slabs in this pattern, my path will reach exactly 8 metres long.' Explain why Mr Anderson is wrong.

NNS links

- Explain methods and reasoning about numbers, orally and in writing.
- Reason about shape.

Solution

a) 160 cm

b) 280 cm

c) 20 slabs

d) Continuing the pattern will not see the path equal exactly 8 m – it will measure either 7·6 metres or 8·4 metres long.

(20) Cycle Hire

Cycle hire	
Adult (up to 3 hours):	£9
Adult (whole day):	£13
Children U-12 (up to 3 hours):	£5
Children U-12 (whole day):	£8

Problem

a) What is the cost of 3 adults each hiring a cycle for a whole day?

b) Mr and Mrs Garrett and their 2 children hire bicycles from 2.00 p.m. to 4.00 p.m. How much do the family pay?

c) A group of adults hire bicycles for $2\frac{1}{2}$ hours. They pay £65 and receive £2 change. How many people are in the group?

d) Mr Bagley takes a group of children from his primary school cycling for a whole day. He has exactly £100 to spend on bicycle hire for himself and the children. How many children can he afford to take?

NNS links

■ Use all four operations to solve word problems involving money.

Solution

a) £39

b) £28

c) 7

d) 10

(21) Water Bottles

Problem

Mineral water is sold in bottles each holding 300 ml. Each bottle costs 45p.

a) Russell spends £2·25 on mineral water. How many bottles does he buy?

b) Jackie drinks a bottle of mineral water a day. How much mineral water does she drink in a week?

c) Russell goes to the supermarket where 12 bottles of mineral water are on offer at £4·45. Jackie buys 12 bottles for 45p each. How much more than Russell does Jackie spend?

d) Harriet buys some bottles of mineral water for 45p each. She gives the shopkeeper a £10 note and receives 10p change. How many bottles does she buy?

NNS links

■ Use all four operations to solve word problems involving money.

Solution

a) 5 bottles

b) 2·1 litres

c) 95p

d) 22 bottles

(22) Jigsaw Fun

Problem

Mark bought a 400-piece jigsaw puzzle for £6·95.

a) Mark paid for the jigsaw with a £10 note. How much change did he receive?
b) In his first attempt he fitted 83 pieces. How many pieces did he have left?
c) After his second attempt Mark had 102 pieces remaining. How many pieces did he fit in his second attempt?
d) Mark's father bought a 600-piece jigsaw for £8·99 and fitted exactly $\frac{1}{4}$ of the pieces in his first attempt. How many pieces did he have left?
e) The largest jigsaw in the store had 1500 pieces and cost £14·99. Mark said that this jigsaw costs about 1p a piece. Is he correct? Explain your answer.

NNS links

■ Explain methods and reasoning about numbers, orally and in writing.
■ Use all four operations to solve word problems in 'real life'.

Solution

a) £3·05
b) 317
c) 215
d) 450
e) Yes – £14·99 = 1499p. 1499p for 1500 pieces is about 1p a piece.

---

(23) Letter Values

Problem

To find the 'letter value' of a town or city, give each letter its value from the alphabet as below, then add all the values together.

A = 1; B = 2; C = 3; D = 4; E = 5 etc.

So, L   O   N   D   O   N

      12 + 15 + 14 + 4 + 15 + 14 = 84.

a) What are the 'letter values' of these cities: Liverpool; Oxford?

b) Which of these cities have 'letter values' which are odd numbers: Lincoln; Cambridge; Exeter; Cardiff?

c) Find the 'letter values' of these cities, then put the cities into the correct place in the Venn diagram: Bristol; Leeds; Plymouth; Newcastle.

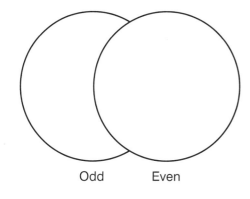

Odd   Even

NNS links

■ Solve mathematical problems or puzzles, recognise and explain patterns and relationships, generalise and predict. Suggest extensions by asking 'What if …?'

Solution

a) 124; 82

b) Lincoln (79), Exeter (77) and Cardiff (47)

c)

Bristol   Plymouth

Leeds   Newcastle

Odd   Even

99

(24) Visit to the Theme Park

Problem

240 pupils from Grove Primary School went on an outing to the theme park in Hendy.

a) 96 of the children were boys. How many girls were there?

b) The coach left at 8.30 a.m. and returned to school at 5.30 p.m. How long did the trip last?

c) The school needed to take one adult for every 15 children going on the trip. How many adults did the school require?

d) The coaches hired by the school could each carry 45 passengers. How many coaches were needed for the trip?

e) All the spare seats were on the last coach. 'Over half the seats on the last coach will be empty,' said Lucy. Is she correct? Explain your answer.

NNS links

- Explain methods and reasoning about numbers, orally and in writing
- Use all four operations to solve word problems in 'real life'.

Solution

a) 144 girls

b) 9 hours

c) 16 adults

d) 6 coaches

e) No – 14 out of 45 seats will be empty. This is under half.

(25) Count the Spots

Problem

Lisa had a collection of plastic discs.

The red discs each had 3 spots on them.

The blue discs each had 4 spots and the yellow discs 5 spots.

a) Lisa put 4 yellow discs and 5 blue discs in the bag. What was the total number of spots?

b) Lisa put only red and yellow discs into the bag. She then picked out 5 discs and counted the spots. There were 21 spots altogether. How many red discs and how many yellow discs were in the bag?

c) Next time, Lisa used red and blue discs only. There were 7 discs in total and 26 spots in total. How many red discs and how many blue discs were there?

d) Finally, Lisa placed red, blue and yellow discs in the bag. When she counted the spots there were 37 altogether. Find three ways she could have made this total.

NNS links

- Solve mathematical problems or puzzles, recognise and explain patterns and relationships, generalise and predict. Suggest extensions by asking 'What if …?'

Solution

a) 40

b) 2 reds and 3 yellows

c) 2 reds and 5 blues

d) 5 yellows and 3 blues; 6 yellows, 1 blue and 1 red; 3 yellows, 1 blue and 6 reds; 4 blues and 7 reds amongst others

(26) Logical Thinking

Problem

a) What does each symbol stand for:

   # + # = 24

   # + $ = 19

   $ + £ = 18

b) Now try these:

   ❑ + ◯ = 17

   ▲ + ❑ = 15

   ◯ + ◯ = 18

c) Here, letters stand for numbers. Again, find the value of each letter:

   B + C = 23

   C − B = 3

NNS links

▪ Solve mathematical problems or puzzles, recognise and explain patterns and relationships, generalise and predict. Suggest extensions by asking 'What if …?'

Solution

a) # = 12, $ = 7, £ = 11

b) ❑ = 8, ◯ = 9, ▲ = 7

c) B = 10, C = 13

---

(27) In My Head

Problem

a) I am thinking of an even number that is between 20 and 40. It is a multiple of 3 and also a multiple of 9. What is my number?

b) The number I have in my head is an even number more than 40 but less than 60. It is not a multiple of 4 but is a multiple of both 6 and 9. What number is in my head?

c) My number is odd – it is less than double 23, more than treble 13, less than half of 86 and more than one fifth of 200. What is my number?

NNS links

▪ Choose and use appropriate number operations and appropriate ways of calculating to solve problems.
▪ Make and investigate a general statement about familiar numbers or shapes by finding examples that satisfy it.

Solution

a) 36

b) 54

c) 41

28 Pick a Number (1)

Use these numbers to answer the questions below.

32	47	238	59	156	37
78	167	94	111	119	

a) Find three numbers that are exactly half of three other numbers above.

b) Which number is $\frac{1}{3}$ of 111?

c) There are four numbers above, which, if I add 18 to them, will make a multiple of 5. Can you find these four numbers?

NNS links

- Choose and use appropriate number operations and appropriate ways of calculating to solve problems.
- Solve mathematical problems or puzzles, recognise and explain patterns and relationships, generalise and predict. Suggest extensions by asking 'What if …?'

Solution

a) 47 (of 94), 78 (of 156), 119 (of 238)

b) 37

c) 32, 47, 37 and 167

29 Pick a Number (2)

Problem

Use these numbers to answer the questions below.

4	58	7	114	6	15
9	87	2	30	5	

a) Which number above is i) $\frac{1}{2}$ of 116 ii) double 57 iii) half way between 2 and 16?

b) Six of the numbers above are factors of 60. Can you find them?

c) If I multiplied 6 by 3 the answer is 18. 18 is a multiple of 9. Which other numbers above, when multiplied by 3, give you a multiple of 9? Show your working.

NNS links

- Choose and use appropriate number operations and appropriate ways of calculating to solve problems.
- Solve mathematical problems or puzzles, recognise and explain patterns and relationships, generalise and predict. Suggest extensions by asking 'What if …?'

Solution

a) i) 58 ii) 114 iii) 9

b) 4, 6, 15, 2, 30 and 5

c) 114, 15, 9, 87, 30

③⓪ Even It Up (1)

Problem

Use only the numbers 1, 2, 3, 4, 5, 6 and 7.

Put each number into one of the boxes below so that the total of the first row equals the total of the second row.

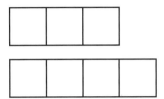

NNS links

■ Solve mathematical problems or puzzles, recognise and explain patterns and relationships, generalise and predict. Suggest extensions by asking 'What if …?'

Solution

7, 6, 1 and 2, 3, 4, 5 (or any combinations where the total of each row is 14)

---

③① Even It Up (2)

Problem

Use only the numbers 1, 2, 3, 4, 5, 6 and 7. Place each into one of the boxes below so that the total of the row and each of the two columns is 12.

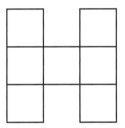

NNS links

■ Solve mathematical problems or puzzles, recognise and explain patterns and relationships, generalise and predict. Suggest extensions by asking 'What if …?'

Solution

2		1
3	4	5
7		6

(or any combinations where each total is 12)

---

③② Even It Up (3)

Problem

Using the numbers 1, 2, 3, 4, 5, 6, 7, 8 and 9, place each into one of the boxes below so that each row totals the same amount.

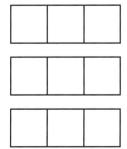

NNS links

■ Solve mathematical problems or puzzles, recognise and explain patterns and relationships, generalise and predict. Suggest extensions by asking 'What if …?'

Solution

9	5	1
8	4	3
7	6	2

(or any combinations where the total of each row is 15)

(33) Cross Country

Problem

The chart shows the finishing times for the Year 5 runners in Parkway School's annual cross-country race.

Runner	Finishing time
Heather	24 minutes 56 seconds
Mitchell	19 minutes 7 seconds
Sophie	21 minutes 18 seconds
Luke	24 minutes 24 seconds
Joanne	20 minutes 31 seconds
Thomas	22 minutes 49 seconds
Jessica	21 minutes 25 seconds

a) Who won the race?

b) Which runner finished immediately in front of Thomas?

c) How many seconds faster than Jessica was Sophie?

d) Which runner finished almost exactly 3 minutes after Jessica?

e) Joanne finished in 20 minutes 31 seconds. How many seconds is this? Show your working.

NNS links

■ Use all four operations to solve word problems involving time.

Solution

a) Mitchell

b) Jessica

c) 7 seconds

d) Luke

e) 1231 seconds

(34) Time Conversions

Problem

1 minute = 60 seconds	1 hour = 60 minutes
1 day = 24 hours	1 week = 7 days
1 year = 12 months, 52 weeks or 365 days	
1 leap year = 366 days	1 decade = 10 years
1 century = 100 years	1 millennium = 1000 years

Use a calculator to work out the following.

a) How many days are in 38 weeks?

b) If 336 hours passed, how many days is this?

c) How many minutes in $12\frac{1}{2}$ hours?

d) Is 1500 minutes more or less than one day? Explain your answer.

e) Christina says that in the 5 years from the beginning of 2000 to the end of 2004 there will have been exactly 1827 days. Can she be correct? Explain your answer.

NNS links

■ Explain methods and reasoning about numbers, orally and in writing
■ Use all four operations to solve word problems involving time.

Solution

a) 266

b) 14

c) 750

d) More (1440 minutes in a day)

e) Yes – the first and fifth years are leap years
$(2 \times 366) + (3 \times 365) = 1827$

(35) Number Rules

Problem

Find the missing numbers in these series. In each case, the rule is given for you.

a) To find the next number, double the previous number.

_____ , 14, 28, 56, _____ , _____ .

b) To find the next number in this series, find half of the previous number.

_____ , 88, _____ , 22, _____ .

c) To find the next number, add 1·3 to the previous number.

_____ , 3·5, 4·8, _____ , 7·4, 8·7, _____ .

d) Each number in this series is $1\frac{1}{2}$ less than the number before it.

_____ , 5, _____ , 2 , _____ , _____ .

NNS links

■ Make and investigate a general statement about familiar numbers or shapes by finding examples that satisfy it.

Solution

a) 7, 112, 224

b) 176, 44, 11

c) 2·2, 6·1, 10(·0)

d) $6\frac{1}{2}$, $3\frac{1}{2}$, $\frac{1}{2}$, −1

---

(36) Bus Stop

Problem

A new bus service between Bagley and Morsham has been set up. Here are the times the buses run:

	Bus A	Bus B	Bus C	Bus D
Bagley	08.30	11.20	14.10	17.30
Denton	08.55	11.45	14.35	17.55
Soulbury	09.30	12.20	15.10	18.30
Alchester	10.00	12.50	15.40	19.00
Morsham	10.40	13.30	16.20	19.40

a) What time does Bus B arrive at Morsham?

b) If I caught the 17.55 bus from Denton, what time would I expect to arrive in Alchester?

c) How long does it take the bus to travel from Denton to Soulbury?

d) Lauren arrives at Soulbury bus station at 18.05. How much longer will she have to wait to catch a bus to Morsham?

e) You need to arrive at Alchester by 1.00 p.m. At what time would you catch the bus from Denton to do this?

f) Sean arrives at Bagley bus station 10 minutes after Bus B has left. How many minutes does he have to wait before Bus C leaves?

NNS links

■ Use all four operations to solve word problems involving time.

Solution

a) 13.30

b) 19.00

c) 35 minutes

d) 25 minutes

e) 11.45

f) 160 minutes

105

37 A Question of Length

Problem

| 10 mm = 1 cm 100 cm = 1 m 1000 m = 1 km |

Use a calculator to work out:

a) How many millimetres in 7 centimetres?

b) How many centimetres in $8\frac{1}{2}$ metres?

c) If I have travelled 16 500 metres, how many kilometres is this?

d) How many millimetres in $5\frac{1}{4}$ metres?

e) Pippa said that if she walks 10 kilometres, she has actually travelled one million centimetres. Is she correct? Explain your answer.

NNS links

■ Explain methods and reasoning about numbers, orally and in writing.
■ Use all four operations to solve word problems involving length, mass or capacity.

Solution

a) 70 mm   b) 850 cm

c) $16\frac{1}{2}$ km   d) 5250 mm

e) Yes – 100 × 1000 cm (100 000 cm) = 1 km.
   100 000 × 10 km = 1 million centimetres.

38 From the Ice Box

Problem

Mrs Minett had just received a new stock of ice creams to sell in her shop. She put the price list up above the freezer.

Ice cream	Price
Juicy Fruity	£1·30
Rocket Stick	£0·85
Super Sundae	£1·55
Ice Slice	£0·65
Double Flake	£1·30
Plain and Simple	£0·45

a) Yasmin and her two friends bought 2 Rocket Sticks and an Ice Slice. How much did they pay in total?

b) What is the difference in cost between the most expensive and the cheapest ice cream?

c) The James family each had a Plain and Simple. Altogether, the bill came to £2·70. How many people were in the James Family?

d) Gordon ordered 2 Super Sundaes and 2 Juicy Fruities. He gave Mrs Minett a £5 note, but it was not enough. How much more does Gordon need to pay Mrs Minett?

d) Melissa decided to treat herself and her six friends to an ice cream. She gave Mrs Minett £6 and received 5p change. All the children had the same type of ice cream. Which one did they have?

NNS links

■ Use all four operations to solve word problems involving money.

Solution

a) £2·35

b) £1·10

c) 6

d) 70p

e) Rocket Stick

(39) Savings

Problem

A group of children from Mr Harrison's class were discussing their savings.

a) 'I save £2·75 each week,' said Alex. How much will Alex save in 20 weeks?

b) 'I save the same amount each month,' said Abigail, 'and in the last 7 months I've saved £92·75.' How much has Abigail saved each month?

c) Charlotte tells Mary-Ann that she is saving up for a new bicycle which costs £120. If she saves £2·50 each week, how long will it take her to save enough to buy the bicycle?

d) 'I put all my spare silver coins in a jar,' said Freddie. 'When I last counted it, I had £8·85.' How many of each coin might he have had?

e) Heather had saved an equal amount each week for 13 weeks; she then took all her money to the shop to buy a pair of trainers. The trainers cost £48·75. How much had Heather saved each week?

NNS links

■ Use all four operations to solve word problems involving money.

Solution

a) £55

b) £13·25

c) 48 weeks

d) Open – answer to include silver coins to the value of £8·85

e) £3·75

---

(40) Missing Numbers

Problem

Use a calculator to find the missing number in each calculation.

a) $18·4 - \underline{\quad\quad} = 5·7$

b) $\underline{\quad\quad} \times 6·7 = 46·9$

c) $19·3 + \underline{\quad\quad} = 76·7$

d) $119·2 \div \underline{\quad\quad} = 14·9$

e) $\underline{\quad\quad} - 8·46 = 23·54$

f) $\underline{\quad\quad} \div 18 = 6·3$

Make sure you check your answers when you have finished.

NNS links

■ Explain methods and reasoning about numbers, orally and in writing.

Solution

a) 12·7

b) 7

c) 57·4

d) 8

e) 32

f) 113·4

(41) True, False or Sometimes True? (1)

Problem

Say whether these statements are always true, sometimes true or never true and explain your answer.

a) If the perimeter of a rectangle is 30 cm, one of the sides is 5 cm.

b) If I add two odd numbers together I make an even number.

c) A pentagon has no right angles.

d) The difference between two even numbers is odd.

e) To multiply a number by 10, you add a '0'.

NNS links

■ Explain methods and reasoning about numbers, orally and in writing.

■ Make and investigate a general statement about familiar numbers or shapes by finding examples that satisfy it.

Solution

(explanations / proofs required)

a) Sometimes true

b) Always true

c) Sometimes true

d) Never true

e) Sometimes true

(42) Back to the Beginning

Problem

a) I think of a number and add 34. The answer is 57. What is my number?

b) Half of a number is 19. What is the number?

c) Stephen doubled his number then subtracted 5. His answer was 31. What number was Stephen thinking of?

d) Tessa's number is half Ben's number. Ben's number is the difference between 18 and 64. What is Tessa's number?

e) I divide the number in my head by 5, then add 11. I finish up with 24. What number is in my head?

f) $\frac{1}{4}$ of Stephanie's number is $\frac{1}{2}$ Joe's number. Joe's number is triple 20. What is Stephanie's number?

NNS links

■ Solve mathematical problems or puzzles, recognise and explain patterns and relationships, generalise and predict. Suggest extensions by asking 'What if …?'

Solution

a) 23

b) 38

c) 18

d) 23

e) 65

f) 120

Tessa has 8 square tiles and arranges them in a rectangle as shown. She says, 'The perimeter of this shape is 12.'

Tessa then rearranges the 8 tiles like this. 'The perimeter is now 14,' she says.

Henry tried rearranging the tiles. This is how he did it.

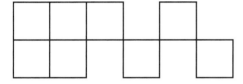

'That's not allowed,' said Tessa. 'Whole sides must be touching to make these shapes, so you can't have something like this either …'

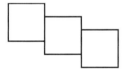

a) Tessa thinks that you cannot make a shape using 8 square tiles that has a perimeter less than 12. Is she correct?

b) What is the largest perimeter you can make using 8 square tiles?

c) Henry says, 'I can make a shape using 8 square tiles, where the perimeter is an odd number.' Is he correct? Show your working.

NNS links

■ Reason about shape.

Solution

a) Yes

b) 18 (8×1)

c) No – all perimeters using 8 tiles will be even. If you start with 8 separate tiles you have a total perimeter of 32. Every time you join one of these tiles to another in making your shape according to the rules, you reduce the total perimeter by an even number because the paired-up sides are no longer part of the perimeter, so you can never finish up with an odd number.

Squares within Squares

Problem

Karl took his hundred square and drew a 3 × 3 square on it like this:

1	2	3	4	5	6	7
11	12	13	14	15	16	17
21	22	23	24	25	26	27
31	32	33	34	35	36	37
41	42	43	44	45	46	47
51	52	53	54	55	56	57
61	62	63	64	65	66	67

He then added the 4 corner numbers in his square:

12 + 14 + 32 + 34 = 92.

a) There are 9 other ways of making 92 by adding 4 numbers in Karl's square. How many can you find?

b) What do you notice about 92 and the middle number in Karl's square?

c) Try drawing another 3 × 3 square somewhere else in your hundred square. Is the pattern still the same?

NNS links

- Explain methods and reasoning about numbers, orally and in writing.
- Solve mathematical problems or puzzles, recognise and explain patterns and relationships, generalise and predict. Suggest extensions by asking 'What if …?'

Solution

a) 12 + 13 + 33 + 34 = 92
13 + 14 + 32 + 33 = 92
14 + 24 + 22 + 32 = 92
12 + 22 + 24 + 34 = 92
33 + 22 + 13 + 24 = 92
13 + 23 + 24 + 32 = 92
13 + 22 + 23 + 34 = 92
14 + 22 + 23 + 33 = 92
12 + 23 + 24 + 33 = 92

b) 92 is 4 times as big as the middle number (4 × 23 = 92)

c) Yes – the pattern is the same wherever you draw the 3 × 3 square.

Problem

Tara took the numbers 1, 2, 3, 4 and 5 and added them together. She made the answer 15. She then added the numbers 1, 2, 3, 4, 5, 6 and 7 together and made 28.

'That's good,' said Carly, 'but there's a much quicker way. Look at the middle number, do a quick multiplication and you have your answer.'

1 2 **3** 4 5 $(1 + 2 + 3 + 4 + 5 = 15)$.

a) What did Carly do to the middle number?

b) Use this method to add the following consecutive numbers:

   i) 1, 2, 3, 4, 5, 6, 7, 8 and 9.

   ii) 11, 12, 13, 14 and 15.

   iii) 23, 24, 25, 26 and 27.

   iv) 26, 27, 28, 29, 30, 31, 32, 33 and 34.

'That's good,' agreed Tara when she had finished, 'but I think it will only work when you have an odd number of numbers. Is there a way of doing the same sort of thing when you have an even number of numbers like 1, 2, 3, 4, 5 and 6?'

c) Look at the two middle numbers in this string:

   1 2 **3** **4** 5 6

   Can you find a method of working out the total of 1, 2, 3, 4, 5 and 6 using the two middle numbers? Does this work with other sets of consecutive numbers?

   Test bigger strings with a calculator.

NNS links

- Explain methods and reasoning about numbers, orally and in writing.
- Make and investigate a general statement about familiar numbers or shapes by finding examples that satisfy it.

Solution

a) She multiplied it by 5 (there are 5 numbers in the 'string')

b) i) $5 \times 9 = 45$
   ii) $13 \times 5 = 65$
   iii) $25 \times 5 = 125$
   iv) $30 \times 9 = 270$

c) Add the 2 middle numbers together and multiply by half the numbers in the 'string' $(7 \times 3 = 21)$ or average the middle numbers (3·5) and multiply by however many numbers there are in the 'string' (6). Yes – it works for all consecutive number strings where there is an even number of numbers.

46 At the Youth Club

Problem

a) Jenny and Christie were talking about their pocket money. 'My brother gets twice as much as me,' explained Jenny. If Jenny's brother received £5 a week, how much did Jenny get?

b) Christie said she got three times as much as her younger sister. If Christie's pocket money is £4·50 a week, how much does her younger sister receive?

c) If Jenny's brother's pocket money went up to £7 a week, how much should Jenny then receive if her brother gets twice as much as she does?

d) For every boy at the youth club on Wednesday evening there were 3 girls. If there were 9 boys at the club on Wednesday evening, how many girls were there?

e) On Friday evening, for every 2 boys at the club there were 5 girls. If there were 35 girls present, how many boys were there?

f) At the youth club disco on Saturday, there were twice as many girls as boys present. If there were 75 people altogether at the dance, how many girls were there?

NNS links

■ Use all four operations to solve word problems involving numbers in 'real life'.
■ Use all four operations to solve word problems involving money.

Solution

a) £2·50

b) £1·50

c) £3·50

d) 27 girls

e) 14 boys

f) 50 girls

47 Party Time

Problem

The corner shop sold three different types of fizzy drinks in three different sized bottles:

Orange	Lemonade	Cherry Pop
300 ml	600 ml	900 ml
50p	75p	£1

a) Georgina has £2·50 to spend. She could buy 2 bottles of Cherry Pop (£2) and 1 bottle of Fizzy Orange (50p) with her money. Can you find 4 other ways she could spend exactly £2·50 on these drinks?

b) Rhys and Aaron decided to have a party at which they would mix up 3000 ml of fizzy drink into a fizzy cocktail. Aaron looked at the bottles in the shop and decided he would buy 2 bottles of Cherry Pop (1800 ml) and 2 bottles of Lemonade (2 × 600 ml) for the party. If the boys bought at least 1 bottle of Cherry Pop for their cocktail, how many other combinations of drinks can you find?

NNS links

■ Use all four operations to solve word problems involving money.
■ Use all four operations to solve word problems involving length, mass or capacity.

Solution

Four from: a) 5 × FO; 3 × FO and 1 × CP; 2 × FO and 2 × L; 2 × L and 1 × CP; 1 × CP and 3 × FO

8 combinations: b) 3 × CP and 1 × FO; 2 × CP and 4 × FO; 2 × CP, 1 × L and 2 × FO; 1 × CP, 1 × FO and 3 × L; 1 × CP, 2 × L, 3 × FO; 1 × CP, 3 × L and 1 × FO; 1 × CP and 7 × FO; 1 × CP, 1 × L and 5 × FO

Problem

Mr and Mrs Mustard were selling hot dogs and burgers at the cricket match.

Menu	
Beefburgers	£1·75
Cheeseburgers	£1·95
Baconburgers	£2·25
Hot Dogs	£1·10
Jumbo Hot Dogs	£1·60
Cold Drinks	£0·65

a) All the burgers were sold in round bread rolls. Mr and Mrs Mustard brought 100 round rolls with them. By lunchtime, they had sold 27 beefburgers, 32 cheeseburgers and 13 baconburgers. How many round rolls had they left?

b) How much did Mr and Mrs Mustard take from the sale of cheeseburgers by lunchtime?

c) Kelly ordered 3 jumbo hot dogs and 2 cold drinks.

   i) What is the smallest value note she could have paid with?

   ii) How much change did she receive?

d) During the afternoon, Mr and Mrs Mustard took £47·30 from the sale of hot dogs and £57·75 from the sale of beefburgers. How many hot dogs and how many beefburgers did they sell during this period?

NNS links

◼ Use all four operations to solve word problems involving money.

Solution

a) 28

b) £62·40

c) i) A £10 note ii) £3·90

d) 43 hot dogs and 33 beefburgers

(49) Egg Boxes

(49)

Problem

Eggs are sold in the supermarket in boxes of 6 (small), 12 (medium) or 24 (large).

a) How many small boxes will be needed to hold 50 eggs?

b) How many eggs are there in 14 full medium-sized boxes?

c) 16 large boxes are full of eggs. How many medium-sized boxes would be needed to hold the same number?

d) 18 small and 13 medium-sized boxes were inspected and it was found that a quarter of the eggs in these were either cracked or broken. How many eggs in these boxes were not cracked or broken?

e) How many large boxes can be filled from 300 eggs?

NNS links

■ Use all four operations to solve word problems involving numbers in 'real life'.

Solution

a) 9

b) 168

c) 32

d) 198

e) 12

---

(50) A Good Read

Problem

Gregory was reading a book about a boy who was a wizard. The book had 640 pages.

a) After 4 days, Gregory was exactly a quarter of the way through the book. How many pages had he read?

b) If he had read the same number of pages on each of the first four days, how many pages would Gregory have read by day three?

c) Gregory read for a long time on the fifth day and when he put the book down he was on page 247. How many more pages must he read to reach the middle of the book?

d) By the beginning of day 10, Gregory had reached page 420. At the end of day 11 he was on page 510. He read 20 more pages on day 10 than he did on day 11. How many pages did Gregory read on day 10?

e) Because he had lots of homework the following week, Gregory did not finish the book until day 20. Gregory worked out that if he had read the same number of pages on each of the 20 days, he would have read 32 pages a day. Is he correct? Explain your answer.

NNS links

■ Explain methods and reasoning about numbers, orally and in writing.
■ Use all four operations to solve word problems involving numbers in 'real life'.

Solution

a) 160

b) 120

c) 73

d) 55

e) Yes – $640 \div 20 = 32$

51 School Concert

Problem

Seats were set out in the school hall for the end of term concert. The seats were placed in 16 rows with 15 seats in each row. Tickets for the concert cost £3·50 each.

a) On the first night, 193 people attended. How many empty seats were there?

b) How much was taken in ticket sales on the first night?

c) On the second night, $\frac{1}{4}$ of the seats remained unsold. How many people attended on the second night?

d) On the third night, $\frac{1}{3}$ of rows 7 and 11 were empty while 9 of the seats in row 15 were unsold. All the other rows were full. What was the attendance on the third night?

e) On the fourth and final night, £829·50 was taken in ticket sales. How many seats remained unsold on the final night?

NNS links

■ Choose and use appropriate number operations and appropriate ways of calculating to solve problems.

■ Use all four operations to solve word problems involving numbers in 'real life'.

Solution

a) 47

b) £675·50

c) 180

d) 221

e) 3

---

52 On the Slate

Problem

A builder is putting slates on a roof. The slates are 20 cm long and each slate must overlap the one before by 5 cm as shown.

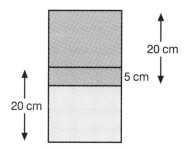

a) If 2 slates are placed on the roof as in the diagram, what will the total length be?

b) If a third slate is added to the line, what will the total length now be?

c) How many slates will need to be laid to make a line measuring exactly 95 cm?

d) If slates 30 cm long with an overlap of 10 cm were used, how many slates will be needed to cover 1 metre of roof?

NNS links

■ Reason about shape.

Solution

a) 35 cm

b) 50 cm

c) 6 slates

d) 5 slates

Problem

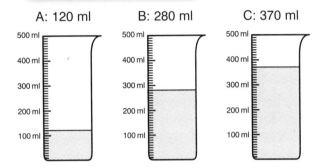

A: 120 ml   B: 280 ml   C: 370 ml

a) 150 ml of water is added to Cylinder A. What is the new level of water?

b) How much water needs to be taken out of Cylinder B to leave 90 ml?

c) Half the water in Cylinder C is removed. How much water remains?

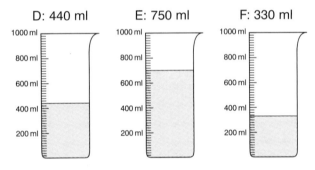

D: 440 ml   E: 750 ml   F: 330 ml

d) How much water needs to be added to Cylinder D to make it equal to Cylinder E?

e) Half the water in Cylinder E is removed. How much more needs to be taken out so that the amount remaining is equal to Cylinder F?

f) The amount of water in Cylinder F is doubled. How much more needs to be added to equal 1 litre?

NNS links

■ Use all four operations to solve word problems involving length, mass or capacity.

Solution

a) 270 ml

b) 190 ml

c) 185 ml

d) 310 ml

e) 45 ml

f) 340 ml

Problem

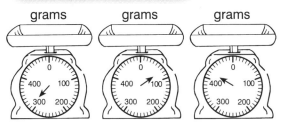

Scale A: 310 g   Scale B: 70 g   Scale C: 420 g

Three children were weighing various amounts of flour in their cookery lesson.

a) How much flour needs to be added to Scale B to equal 150 g?

b) 240 g of flour is taken out of Scale C. What mass of flour remains?

c) Half the flour in Scale A is removed. What mass of flour is left in the scale?

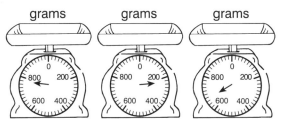

Scale D: 780 g   Scale E: 230 g   Scale F: 670 g

d) What is the difference in the mass of flower in Scale F and the mass of flour in Scale D?

e) If the flour in Scale E was added to the flour in Scale F, what would be the new mass of flour in Scale F?

f) How much flour needs to be added to Scale D to make the mass into 1 kg?

NNS links

■ Use all four operations to solve word problems involving length, mass or capacity.

Solution

a) 80 g

b) 180 g

c) 155 g

d) 110 g

e) 900 g

f) 220 g

Problem

Below is part of a calendar from April 2004. Some of the page is missing.

April 2004

S	M	T	W	T
4	5	6	7	8
11	12	13	14	
18	19	20		
25	26	27		

a) On what day does 15th April fall?

b) Azim's birthday is on the Saturday of the second full week in April. What date is this?

c) Lea went on holiday on Tuesday 13th April and returned 10 days later. Give the day and the date on which she returned.

d) What is the date of the last Sunday in March 2004?

e) Hodditon School breaks up for Easter on Friday 9th April. The pupils have a full two weeks off before returning to school on the following Monday. Give the date on which they return.

f) There are 30 days in April. On what day does the 4th May 2004 fall?

NNS links

■ Use all four operations to solve word problems involving time.

Solution

a) Thursday

b) 17th April

c) Friday 23rd April

d) 28th

e) 26th April

f) Tuesday

Problem

Elliott was studying his new Year 5 school timetable for Mondays.

8.50 a.m.	Registration
9.05 a.m.	Assembly
9.30 a.m.	Maths
10.35 a.m.	Break
11.00 a.m.	Literacy
12.05 p.m.	PE
12.50 p.m.	Lunch
1.45 p.m.	Guided Reading
2.10 p.m.	Music
2.45 p.m.	History
3.30 p.m.	School ends

a) For how many minutes does Monday's literacy lesson last?

b) Elliott had a dental appointment on Monday. He left school at 12.30 p.m. and returned 2 hours later in the middle of which lesson?

c) In total, how many minutes do the children get for morning break and lunch?

d) Last Monday's assembly had been extended by 15 minutes because there was a visiting speaker, making that day's maths lesson shorter. How long was last Monday's maths lesson?

e) Calculate, in hours and minutes, the amount of time pupils spend at school each day from the beginning of registration to the time school ends.

NNS links

■ Use all four operations to solve word problems involving time.

Solution

a) 65 minutes

b) Music

c) 80 minutes

d) 50 minutes

e) 6 hours 40 minutes

57 Car Boot Sale

Problem

Stuart's football team decided to try to raise money by selling old items of kit at the car boot sale which was held every Sunday morning behind the market place. Stuart's dad and three of the other parents agreed to take their cars along. They put their price lists out on the tables.

Practice Footballs £3·50	Football Shirts £3·25

Shorts £1·50	Socks 85p/pair	Boots £2·50–£6·50

a) Stuart's first customer bought a football shirt, a pair of shorts and a pair of socks. How much did he have to pay?

b) Martin was not doing so well. In the first hour he sold only 3 pairs of socks and then spent 95p of his takings on an ice cream. How much did Martin have left?

c) Jake came to the sale with a £10 note. He bought a pair of boots for £3·75 – what could he have bought with the money he had left?

d) The boys eventually made £13·50 from the sale of shorts. How many pairs did they sell?

e) It cost each of the four parents £6·50 to bring their cars to the sale. Altogether, the team took £67·25. After giving the parents their entry fees back, how much profit had they made?

NNS links

- Use all four operations to solve word problems involving money.

Solution

a) £5·60

b) £1·60

c) Any goods up to the value of £6·25

d) 9 pairs

e) £41·25

Problem

A new sandwich shop was set up on the High Street. This is how it advertised its stock:

Main fillings	(Ham, turkey, cheese or tuna): 95p each	
Main fillings	(Beef, prawn or salmon): £1·15 each	
Other fillings	(Tomato, onion or cucumber): 20p each	
Extras	(Horseradish, mustard, pickle): 15p each	
Baguette:	45p	
Bread Roll:	35p	
Sandwich:	25p	

a) Grace ordered a turkey and tomato roll. How much did she pay?

b) Tom was feeling hungry. 'I'd like a ham and cheese baguette with onion and tomato, please,' he said. What change did he receive from a £5 note?

c) Elizabeth ordered 4 tuna and cucumber sandwiches, while Michelle bought 3 beef and mustard baguettes. Who spent the most and by how much?

d) The shop took £7 on Tuesday morning from the sale of bread rolls only. How many bread rolls did they sell during this time?

e) Stacey and Ashton had £3·50 between them for their lunch. What might they have bought from the Sandwich Shop with this money?

NNS links

■ Use all four operations to solve word problems involving money.

Solution

a) £1·50

b) £2·25

c) Elizabeth by 35p (£5·60 / £5·25)

d) 20

e) Open

Redgrove School held a sponsored run to raise money for some new computers. Here is part of Harry and Jamil's sponsor forms.

Harry

Sponsor	Amount/Lap
Mrs Abbot	£1·00
Tom Johnson	30p
Lisa Kelly	75p
Mum and Dad	£1·50
Keith Hiatt	5p
Cory Gould	40p

Jamil

Sponsor	Amount/Lap
Mum and Dad	£2
Lucy Grant	10p
Angela McCann	35p
Mr and Mrs Rich	40p
Nigel Rice	£1·25
Leroy Appiah	60p

Harry managed 13 laps of the school field.

a) How much sponsor money did Harry's mum and dad have to pay?

b) Lisa Kelly only had a £10 note when Harry asked for his sponsor money. Was it enough? Explain your answer.

c) Mr and Mrs Rich had to pay Jamil £6·40 after his run. How many laps did Jamil complete?

d) Angela McCann gave Jamil £3 and said she would pay him the rest the next day. How much sponsor money did she still owe him?

e) Altogether, the sponsored run raised £2671. New computers cost £980 each. How much more money will the school need to raise to buy 3 new computers?

■ Use all four operations to solve word problems involving money.

a) £19·50

b) Yes – 13 × 75p = £9·75

c) 16 laps

d) £2·60

e) £269

Problem

The new mobile telephone company, Chataway, announced its new rates.

Period	Time	Rate
Mon–Fri Day Time	8.01 am – 6.00 p.m.	20p a minute
Mon–Fri Evenings	6.01 pm – 11.00 p.m.	12p a minute
Mon–Fri Night Time	11.01 pm – 7.59 a.m.	6p a minute
Weekends (Sat 8 a.m. – Mon 8 a.m.)	All times	12p a minute

a) Adrian rang his friend Brian on Saturday evening. The call lasted 6 minutes. How much did he have to pay?

b) Clarissa spent 16 minutes on her phone on Wednesday night, beginning at 11.15 p.m. What did her call cost?

c) Mrs Gibbs made a business call at 2.15 p.m. on Tuesday. The call cost her £2·80. How long did her call last?

d) Annie's weekend bill for last month came to exactly £12. For how many weekend minutes was Annie on her phone last month?

e) John spends 12 minutes on his phone during Friday lunchtime. Glyn waits until 6.15 p.m. on Friday evening and makes a call costing the same amount. For how many minutes did Glyn's call last?

NNS links

- Use all four operations to solve word problems involving money.
- Use all four operations to solve word problems involving time.

Solution

a) 72p

b) 96p

c) 14 minutes

d) 100 minutes

e) 20 minutes

61 At the Round Pound Shop

Problem

At the Round Pound Shop, everything costs exactly £1, £2, £3, etc. There are no pennies involved at all.

a) A book and a video cost £10.
A book and a CD cost £9.
2 videos cost £14.
What is the cost of: a book; a video; a CD?

b) A football and a cricket set cost £12.
A football and a hockey stick cost £14.
A cricket set and a hockey stick cost £18.
What is the cost of: a football; a cricket set; a hockey stick?

c) Computer Game A costs twice as much as Computer Game B. Computer Game B costs twice as much as Computer Game C. Altogether they cost £35. What does each computer game cost?

NNS links

■ Use all four operations to solve word problems involving money.

Solution

a) Book £3; Video £7; CD £6

b) Football £4; Cricket set £8; Hockey stick £10

c) Game A £20; Game B £10; Game C £5

---

62 True, False or Sometimes True? (2)

Problem

Say whether these statements are always true, sometimes true or never true and explain your answer.

a) Multiplying two odd numbers together gives you an odd number.

b) If you cut an oblong in half, you will make two squares.

c) Adding three odd numbers together gives you an even number.

d) A hexagon has six lines of symmetry.

e) Doubling a number and adding 1 gives you an odd number.

NNS links

■ Explain methods and reasoning about numbers, orally and in writing.
■ Make and investigate a general statement about familiar numbers or shapes by finding examples that satisfy it.

Solution

(explanations/proofs required)

a) Always true

b) Sometimes true

c) Never true

d) Sometimes true

e) Always true

(63) Number Pairs

Problem

Find a pair of numbers with:

a) A total of 8 and a product of 15.

b) A difference of 7 and a total of 23.

c) A product of 27 and a difference of 6.

d) A sum of 30 and a product of 200.

e) A difference of 12 and a sum of 40.

f) A difference of 1 and a product of 42.

g) A total of 20, a difference of 12 and a product of 64.

NNS links

■ Solve mathematical problems or puzzles, recognise and explain patterns and relationships, generalise and predict. Suggest extensions by asking 'What if …?'

Solution

a) 3 and 5

b) 8 and 15

c) 3 and 9

d) 10 and 20

e) 14 and 26

f) 6 and 7

g) 4 and 16

(64) Sensible or Silly?

Problem

Length – millimetres, centimetres, metres, kilometres.

Mass – grams, kilograms.

Capacity – millilitres, litres.

Say whether you think these statements are sensible or silly. Where you think the statement is silly, say what units you would use instead.

You would measure the:

a) Width of your fingernail in metres.

b) Capacity of a swimming pool in litres.

c) Mass of a newspaper in kilograms.

d) Distance from London to Birmingham in metres.

e) Amount of petrol needed to fill a petrol tank in millilitres.

f) Length of a pencil in centimetres.

g) Mass of an adult in grams.

h) Width of a piece of thin wire in millimetres.

i) Mass of a spoonful of sugar in grams.

NNS links

■ Use all four operations to solve word problems involving length, mass or capacity.

Solution

a) Silly (millimetres)

b) Sensible

c) Silly (grams)

d) Silly (kilometres)

e) Silly (litres)

f) Sensible

g) Silly (kilograms)

h) Sensible

i) Sensible

65 Can You Make Me?

Problem

I can use these numbers: 1 2 3 4 and these symbols + − × to make 13 like this:
4 × 3 − 1 + 2.

Now see if you can complete these.

a) Using each of these numbers once only:
   2 4 6 8 and each of these symbols once only: + − × can you make 12?

b) Try using each of these numbers and each of these symbols to make 93: 2 5 8 11 and
   + − ×

c) What about these numbers and symbols?
   7 8 9 10 and + − × to make 35.

d) And finally, use each of these numbers once:
   5 10 15 20 25 and each of these symbols once: + − × ÷ to make 180.

NNS links

■ Solve mathematical problems or puzzles, recognise and explain patterns and relationships, generalise and predict. Suggest extensions by asking 'What if …?'

Solution

a) 6 + 4 (= 10) × 2 (= 20) − 8 = 12

b) 11 + 8 (= 19) × 5 (= 95) − 2 = 93

c) 10 − 7 (= 3) × 9 (= 27) + 8 = 35

d) 25 ÷ 5 (= 5) + 15 (= 20) × 10 (= 200) − 20 = 180

66 Mr Rimmer's New Lawn

Problem

Mr Rimmer is laying a new lawn in his garden. The grass seed he buys costs £3·95 a box and each box contains enough seed to cover 15 square metres of lawn.

a) Mr Rimmer's lawn is 180 square metres in area. How many boxes of grass seed does he need to cover it?

b) How much does Mr Rimmer spend on the grass seed for his new lawn?

c) Mr Rimmer uses a hosepipe and sprinkler to water his new lawn for 90 minutes each evening. He does this for 36 days. For how many hours in total does he water his lawn?

d) Once the lawn is completed, Mr Rimmer decides to put some stepping stones across it so that he can walk to the flower bed on the other side. Stepping stones cost £6·50 each and Mr Rimmer spends a total of £78 on these. How many stepping stones does he buy?

e) Mr Rimmer's lawn is rectangular in shape. If the short sides of his lawn are 12 metres long, what is the length of the longer sides?

NNS links

■ Use all four operations to solve word problems involving numbers in 'real life'.

Solution

a) 12 boxes

b) £47·40

c) 54 hours

d) 12 stepping stones

e) 15 metres

67 Sticker Fun

Problem

Sue and James both collect stickers of famous sports people. They keep their stickers in albums, each of which has 24 pages with 9 stickers completing a page. Sue has been collecting stickers for several years, though James has been collecting for less than a year.

a) By the end of June, James had collected 167 stickers. How many pages of his album had he filled by the end of June?

b) Sue had filled 3 albums and exactly 14 pages of her fourth by the end of June. How many stickers had Sue collected?

c) By December, Sue had collected a further 87 stickers. Has she now collected enough stickers to fill her fourth album? Explain your answer.

d) James had filled 3 pages and had 6 stickers on page 4 of his second album by December. How many stickers had he collected since the end of June?

e) Sue's ambition was to collect 5 full albums of stickers. If she achieves this, how many stickers will she have?

NNS links

■ Use all four operations to solve word problems involving numbers in 'real life'.

Solution

a) 18

b) 774

c) No – she needed to collect a further 90 stickers to complete her fourth album

d) 82 (the remaining 49 on his first album and 33 on his second album)

e) 1080

---

68 Leftovers

Problem

a) Sita buys 11 bars of chocolate, each costing 45p. How much change does she receive from £5?

b) Mr Silk buys 3 kg of potatoes and uses 700 g of them in a stew. What weight of potatoes remains?

c) A piece of string is $2\frac{1}{2}$ metres long. Amy cuts off 95 cm. What length of string is left?

d) Mrs Agassian fills her petrol tank to its 38 litre capacity. Two days later she has used exactly a quarter of the petrol. How much petrol has she left in the tank?

e) Mr Hayes sells sweets in 150 g bags from a container weighing 4 kg. After selling 26 bags of sweets, what weight of sweets remains?

NNS links

■ Use all four operations to solve word problems involving length, mass or capacity.

Solution

a) 5p

b) 2 kg 300 g (or 2300 g)

c) 155 cm (or 1 m 55 cm)

d) $28\frac{1}{2}$ litres

e) 100 g

69 Newspaper Sales

The table below shows how many newspapers three different shops sold during one week in August.

Newsagent	Sun	Mon	Tues	Wed	Thur	Fri	Sat
Mr Nelson	71	46	53	82	66	75	56
Mr Patel	54	69	77	81	56	83	64
Mrs Gough	103	37	48	67	51	60	53

a) Which newsagent sold the greatest number of papers during the week?

b On which 2 days were the same number of newspapers sold?

c) Between which 2 consecutive days did Mrs Gough's sales fall the most?

d) Between which 2 consecutive days did Mr Patel's sales show the greatest increase?

e) On which 3 days was there an equal difference in newspaper sales between Mr Nelson and Mrs Gough?

NNS links

■ Use all four operations to solve word problems involving numbers in 'real life'.

Solution

a) Mr Patel

b) Thursday and Saturday

c) Sunday and Monday

d) Thursday and Friday

e) Wednesday, Thursday and Friday

---

70 Matching Up

Problem

a) Emma has only 2p and 5p pieces in her pocket. She pays for a 30p bar of chocolate, using 9 of her coins. How many of each coin does she use?

b) There were 60 Year 5 pupils at Mossford Primary School. In one games lesson, the Year 5s were split into 5-a-side football teams and 7-a-side netball teams. Altogether, there were 10 teams. How many football and how many netball teams were there?

b) Laima had a 3-sided dice with the numbers 2, 4 and 5 on it. She rolled it 9 times and the total of the numbers was 34. How many of each number did she roll?

NNS links

■ Use all four operations to solve word problems involving numbers in 'real life'.

Solution

a) $5 \times 2p$ and $4 \times 5p$

b) $5 \times$ football and $5 \times$ netball teams

c) $3 \times 2s$, $2 \times 4s$ and $4 \times 5s$

   or $2 \times 2s$, $5 \times 4s$ and $2 \times 5s$

   or 1×2, $8 \times 4s$, no 5s

(71) Temperature Check

Problem

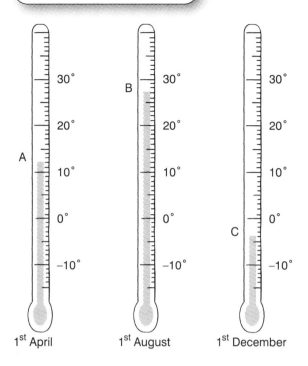

1st April   1st August   1st December

NNS links

■ Use all four operations to solve word problems involving numbers in 'real life'.

Solution

a) 15 degrees

b) 31 degrees

c) 5 degrees

d) 19 degrees

e) 19 degrees

Charmaine recorded the temperature in her garden on 1st April, 1st August and 1st December last year.

a) What was the difference in temperature between 1st April and 1st August?

b) How much lower was the temperature on 1st December than 1st August?

c) By 4th December, the temperature had risen by 9 degrees. What was the temperature on 4th December?

d) The lowest temperature recorded in Moscow in December last year was –23 degrees. How much lower than the temperature in Charmaine's garden on 1st December is this?

e) The highest recorded temperature in Charmaine's garden last December was 13 degrees, while the lowest was –6 degrees. What is the difference between these temperatures? Draw your own temperature scale from 20 degrees to –10 degrees and mark these two temperatures on it.

Lemonade Break

Problem

Lemonade is sold in three different-sized bottles:

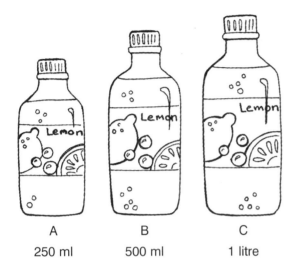

A	B	C
250 ml	500 ml	1 litre

a) Cory drinks 130 ml of lemonade from Bottle B. How much lemonade remains in the bottle?

b) Vicky and Rebecca each drink the same amount from Bottle A. When they have finished, there is 70 ml left. How much does each girl drink?

c) How many 30 ml cups of lemonade can Jane fill from Bottle A?

d) How many times bigger than Bottle A is Bottle C?

e) The lemonade in Bottle C was shared into glasses each containing 80 ml. Eventually there was 40ml left in the bottle. How many glasses was the lemonade shared into?

NNS links

■ Use all four operations to solve word problems involving length, mass or capacity.

Solution

a) 370 ml

b) 90 ml

c) 8

d) 4 times bigger

e) 12

(73) Round Up or Down?

Problem

a) You can fit 12 pencils in a box. If you have 100 pencils, how many boxes can you fill?

b) 83 children are split into 5-a-side teams. How many teams are there?

c) Trays can each hold 8 bedding plants. How many trays will be needed to hold 70 bedding plants?

d) Sticks of rock cost 20p each. Philip has £2·50. How many sticks of rock can he buy?

e) The owner of the tropical fish shop insists on no more than 18 fish in a tank. He has 205 fish. How many tanks does he need?

f) Minibuses can each carry 15 people. How many minibuses are needed to transport 200 people?

g) How many lengths of rope, each measuring 80 cm, can be cut from a rope measuring 5 metres?

h) The maximum number of pupils in a class at Oakham School is 30. If there are 410 pupils at the school, what is the minimum number of classes required?

i) It takes 25 minutes to paint a complete fence panel. How many complete fence panels can be painted in 4 hours?

NNS links

■ Use all four operations to solve word problems involving numbers in 'real life'.

Solution

a) 8 b) 16 c) 9 d) 12 e) 12 f) 14 g) 6 h) 14 i) 9

---

(74) Chicken and Mushroom Soup

Problem

These are some of the ingredients needed to make chicken and mushroom soup for 4 people.

> Chicken – 200 g
>
> Mushrooms – 80 g
>
> Water – 300 ml
>
> Sweetcorn – 60 g
>
> Cream – 200 ml

a) This recipe is for 4 people. If you were going to make this soup for 8 people, how much cream would you use?

b) By using 100 g of chicken, 40 g of mushrooms and 30 g of sweetcorn, how many people would you expect your chicken and mushroom soup to serve?

c) If you were making chicken and mushroom soup for 20 people, how much chicken would you expect to use?

d) If the amount of cream in your recipe was increased to 400 ml, how much water would you expect to use?

e) If you wanted to prepare soup for 6 people, what weight of chicken would you buy?

NNS links

■ Use all four operations to solve word problems involving length, mass or capacity.

Solution

a) 400 ml

b) 2

c) 1000 g (1 kg)

d) 600 ml

e) 300 g

75 Spot the Error

Problem

Four of the six statements below are incorrect. Identify which four are incorrect and in each case give the right answer.

a) Maria buys two items costing £2·35 and £3·47. She pays with a £10 note and receives £3·18 change.

b) Programmes for the concert cost £1·25. Jan collects £9·75 from the sale of 7 programmes.

c) $\frac{1}{4}$ of the children in a school stayed to dinner. In all, 32 children stayed to dinner. There were 128 children in the school in total.

d) In a relay race, the times of the 4 runners in Team One were 16·1 seconds, 15·3 seconds, 15·8 seconds and 15·2 seconds. The total time for Team One was 72·4 seconds.

e) A jug holds 3 litres of orange squash. If 15 people each drink 200 ml, the jug will be empty.

f) A regular hexagon has a perimeter of 90 cm. Each side of the hexagon measures 18 cm.

NNS links

■ Use all four operations to solve word problems involving numbers in 'real life'.

Solution

a) Incorrect – the change should be £4·18

b) Incorrect – Jan collects £8·75

c) Correct

d) Incorrect – the total time was 62·4 seconds

e) Correct

f) Incorrect – each side of the hexagon is 15 cm

76 Divisibility Tests

Problem

a) A number is exactly divisible by 5 if the number ends in either '5' or '0.'

Which three of these numbers are exactly divisible by 5?

83   195   47   562   380   75   98

b) A number is exactly divisible by 4 if the last 2 digits will divide exactly by 4.

Which four of these numbers are exactly divisible by 4?

142   254   436   64   86   528   916

c) A number is exactly divisible by 3 if the sum of the digits is divisible by 3.

Which three of these numbers are exactly divisible by 3?

78   145   203   141   83   246   133

d) All these numbers are divisible by 3, 4 or 5. But which are divisible by which?

295   284   231   275   282   219   244

NNS links

■ Make and investigate a general statement about familiar numbers or shapes by finding examples that satisfy it.

Solution

a) 195, 380 and 75

b) 436, 64, 528 and 916

c) 78, 141, 246

d) 295 – 5, 284 – 4, 231 – 3, 275 – 5, 282 – 3, 219 – 3, 244 – 4